TWO SQUARE MILES:
The Heroes of a Small Town

11-14-09

Skip
Thanks for being
a good friend!!
Bill
Hayes

TWO SQUARE MILES:
The Heroes of a Small Town

by

Bill Hayes

With Forward by Melodie Nichols

Cortero Publishing
www.CorteroPublishing.com
An Imprint of Fireship Press

ISBN-13: 978-1-934757-81-9
ISBN-10: 1-934757-81-0

BISAC Subject Headings:

HIS036090 HISTORY / United States / State & Local / Midwest (IA, IL, IN, KS, MI, MN, MO, ND, NE, OH, SD, WI)

BIO000000 BIOGRAPHY & AUTOBIOGRAPHY / General

Address all correspondence to:

Fireship Press, LLC
P.O. Box 68412
Tucson, AZ 85737

Or visit our website at:
www.FireshipPress.com
www.CorteroPublishing.com

1.1

To my best friend and partner,
Barbara Fraser Hayes,
and family.

CONTENTS

Forward by Melodie Nichols i

Preface v

Arts and Entertainment

Dan Carlisle 3
Radio DJ, FM Radio Pioneer

Pam Coutilish (Pam Scott) 7
Director, Playwright, Acting Teacher

David Frezza 9
Actor, Singer, Dancer,

Ken Gardestad 15
Swedish Song Writer and Architect

Christina Kokubo 21
Movie and TV actress

Robert McKee 23
Broadway Actor, Screenwriter, Lecturer

Jason Mulheisen 27
Movie and TV Actor

Daniel Scanlon 29
Illustrator, Cartoonist, Movie Animator

Angeline Squires 31
International Dancing Star

Terri Turner 35
Miss Michigan Teen USA 1986

Al Terwilliger 37
Actor, Singer, Dancer, Inventor

Victoria Rose Zalewski 41
Puppet Fabricator

Business

Robert Birch 47
Industrial Developer

William D. Morean 51
Co-owner of Jabil Circuits

Beth-Ann Morean 53
Co-owner of Jabil Circuits

Stephan Ross 55
European Textile Entrepreneur

Civic Leaders

Janet Crawford (Lusk) 59
Development Coordinator -
Detroit Institute for Children

Edward Luttenberger 61
Board President -
National Vietnam War Museum

Paul Raine 67
Attorney and Co-founder
of the Greater Detroit Free-Net

Fr. Simon Stark 71
Missionary to Africa

Teri Takai 73
Chief Information Officer State of California

Law

Kyle Hayes 77
National Police Officers Hall of Fame

Bristol Hunter 79
Judge

David Hunter 83
Author and Environmental Lawyer

Military

Edith Davis 87
Pioneering Women's Army Corps Officer

Herbert "Bud" Trexler 91
Army Commander, West Point Professor

Sports

Mark Campbell 97
Tight End — National Football League

Marty Clary 99
Pitcher — Atlanta Braves

Tim Gleason 101
Defenseman — National Hockey League
Ray Hayes 103
Defensive Tackle — National Football League
Member of the 1968 Super Bowl Champion,
New York Jets
Andy Helmuth 105
Drafted by Chicago Blackhawks
Jon Janson 107
Offensive Tackle — National Football League
Tom Joyce 109
Pitcher — Chicago White Sox system
Thomas Morgan 111
Olympic Sports Medicine
Frank Niedowicz 115
Pitcher/Outfielder —
Philadelphia Athletics system
Mary Olsen 117
Two time Big-10 Individual
Gymnastics Champion
Gary Sabaugh 119
Pro Wrestling Federation
Heavyweight Champion
Joseph Sade 121
1976 Olympic Wrestler
Stanley Somers 123
Pitcher — Philadelphia Athletics
Bill Stewart 125
Outfielder — Kansas City Athletics
Brian Woltman 127
Third Baseman — Houston Astros system

Writing and Publishing

Matt Crossman 131
Associate Editor — Sporting News Magazine
Molly Glad 133
Childrens Writer

Jeff Gordon 135
Sports Columnist, TV & Radio talk show host

Tom Grundner 137
Author, Publisher

Clawson to Clawson

Robert Acton 143
CHS Teacher, Coach, Friend

Whitney Hames 147
CHS Teacher

James Hunter 149
Dentist

Steven McClelland 151
Physician

Frederick Reid 153
Physician

Clair Wilson Volk 155
CHS Teacher

Clawson to Clawson Teachers 157

Notables

Valdor "Les" Haglund 161
Father of 2008 Miss America
Kristen Haglund

Arthur Sunquest 163
Friend of the Clawson Police Department

The Ullman Quads 165
Quadruplets born in Clawson

The VanderVen Brothers 167
Researchers, College Professors, Authors

In Remembrance

World War I 171

World War II 172

Korean War 179

VietnamWar 180

About the Author 185

FORWARD

The city of Clawson, Michigan occupies an area of roughly 2.4 square miles and lies about six miles north of the once-bustling city of Detroit. First settled in 1823, what began as a rural crossroads at the intersection of Main Street (Livernois) and 14 Mile Road has grown to be a city of both forward-looking progress and deeply rooted traditions.

The name "Clawson" first appeared on the map about 1880, when the first official Post Office was established. The area was then little more than a country crossroads, with a general store and a steam-powered sawmill. Houses and farms dotted the countryside, with those north of 14 Mile Road lying in Troy Township, and those to the south were in Royal Oak Township.

Beginning in 1899, the Detroit United Railway (DUR) began operations through Clawson. The swift and quiet electric trains zipped up Main Street, offering transportation south to Royal Oak and Detroit, or north through Rochester. The speed and ease of transit made the Clawson area accessible to men working in Detroit, and a "bedroom community" began to grow, as farms were subdivided and new housing developments were begun.

Clawson was incorporated as a village in 1920. By 1924, the population numbered 3,000, and the growing village boasted three churches, two newspapers, three schools, and was served by both electric and telephone services. The village continued to grow rapidly during the 1920s; in one year alone, 500 new homes were built. Its wide open spaces appealed to families weary of the crowds and noise of the city, while still offering easy access to jobs and businesses in Royal Oak and Detroit.

More businesses began to serve the demands of the growing population, and in 1925 the Clawson State Savings Bank was opened on the corner of 14 Mile and Main Street. By the late 1920s, old wooden structures were being replaced with modern brick and stone buildings, most of which still stand, and Clawson was proud to be known as the "Pivot of Progress."

A library was opened in 1929, in a home donated by the Blair family. The current library building is on the site of the old homestead. During the Depression, the library was temporarily closed, as the village could not afford to pay a librarian. The building continued to be used as a classroom for women's handicrafts, which were sold to help support their families, as well as being donated to the needy. Food for needy residents was also distributed from the library during those difficult years. Schools reduced their classes to half days; the Clawson State Savings Bank was forced to close; and electric streetlights were turned off to save money. Train service was discontinued when the DUR, under pressure from a reduction in passengers and a generally poor economy, went bankrupt.

Recovery was slow, but certain. In 1940, the year Clawson was incorporated as a city, the population stood at 4,000. By 1955, it had grown to about 10,500, twice what it had been in 1950. There were eight churches, seven public schools, forty-eight acres of park land, and the library held over 5,000 volumes. There were 10 miles of paved roads (about a quarter of the town), an eight-man police department, and a volunteer fire department with two trucks and fifteen men. Clawson was still a great place to live and raise a family. The 1955 Polk directory, while extolling the virtues of the little burg and its paved highways, gives reasons for this: "Property values are not too high for the working man who can locate here and be employed either in Detroit or Pontiac. The rural atmosphere and the proximity to the beautiful lakes and state parks in this vicinity are factors that the home-owner and lover of the great outdoors will consider when locating in this area. There is no city or village so advantageously located in the north Woodward Avenue district, and this will be an important factor in the Clawson of the future."

Throughout the 60s and 70s, Clawson experienced political and social growing pains, including compliance with Urban Renewal guidelines that placed concrete "tombstones" [1] along down-

[1] These were concrete barriers on the sidewalks about 14" square and 30 inches high, placed about 10 feet apart along the curbs on Main Street. They looked like tombstones, and were very controversial.

town streets and changed parking patterns. One resident claimed there were enough of them to write "Merry Christmas" using one tombstone for each letter. In 1970, Clawson's population peaked with 17,500 residents, and over 4,000 students attending the public schools.

During the intervening years, businesses came and went, but the brick and stone buildings remained, ready for new tenants and the new century. By 2000, the population was 12,732, and the downtown area was beginning to experience a revitalization that continues today.

A number of remarkable people have called Clawson their home. Teachers, attorneys, physicians, artists, athletes, inventors and other Clawson alumni have distinguished themselves in their respective fields, giving Clawson a rich and varied résumé of outstanding achievers.

The people in this book represent a cross-section of Clawsonites who have excelled beyond the ordinary in their achievements. It is hoped their efforts will inspire others to push themselves toward excellence in their chosen path.

From its rural beginnings, through the turbulent decades of the Depression, World War II and the subsequent booms and busts of fortune, Clawson has remained, foremost, a hometown. It offers the amenities of a city while preserving the atmosphere of a small town. It is truly the "Little City with a Big Heart."

Melodie Nichols
June 2009

PREFACE

Growing up and working in Clawson made me realize that, for a town of only 2.4 square miles, we seem to have a large number of people who have accomplished noteworthy, honorable and sometimes even heroic things. I think it is important to point out to the young people of the community that, even though they come from a small town, they too can accomplish great things with hard work and dedication towards a goal.

The selection criteria I am using in this book is that the person had to have lived in town part of the time growing up, or lived in another town and went to school in Clawson. Also they had to have done something noteworthy, unique, or heroic in their lives. I am certain that I only have a partial list of people and there are many others that qualify. I have not listed politicians or city employees as they would be the subject of a different book.

I have also listed the Clawson people that died in World War I, World War II, Korean War and the Vietnam War. As of today's date, I am not aware of anyone that has died in Desert Storm, Iraq or the Afghanistan Wars. The list for World War II was hard to compile, and I am certain it is not complete because the information for most of it came from memorial lists and newspaper accounts which are very hard to obtain.

Another list contains names of people that grew up in town and came back later to teach. The list I have are the people that are teaching at this moment in Clawson or taught here for a substantial portion of their careers.

I would like to thank Melodie Nichols, Curator of Clawson Historical Museum, and retired Curator Deloris Kumler for all their help. I would also like to thank Bob Acton, Shirley Dittmar Wilson,

John Dickinson, Bill Wentz, Bristol Hunter, Luella Dreon Joyce, Beverly Serre Raine and many others—too numerous to mention—for all their help.

If someone feels that there is a person who is not in this book and meets the criteria, please pass the information on to me: Bill Hayes, C/O Clawson Historical Museum, 41 Fisher Ct., Clawson, Michigan 48017. Send me their name, why they should be on the list, and your name, address, phone number and email address so I can contact you.

I wouldn't be surprised if there were enough names to fill a second book.

Bill Hayes
July, 2009

ARTS AND ENTERTAINMENT

Dan Carlisle

CHS 1963

Radio DJ

FM Radio Pioneer

In April 2009, Dan wrote:

I was born Sept 9, 1943, at Mitchell Field, Army Air Corp Bomber base, Long Island, New York.

I moved with my family to a small two bedroom bungalow at 528 Roth Street. My parents lived in that house for more than 50 years. The homes were all brand new in 1949 and I attended the little country kindergarten school across from what is now Clawson Junior High School. After second grade I was enrolled at Guardian Angels School on 14 mile Road. I finished 8th grade and transferred back to Clawson public school until I graduated in 1963.

After graduating I only knew that I did not want to wind up in a factory for the rest of my life. I attended Ferris State for a year and a half and came home with a decent grade point average but little enthusiasm for returning to the middle of Western Michigan.

I had always been in love with radio and while attending Oakland Community College I met the son of an ABC radio executive who worked at WXYZ out in Southfield. At that time WXYZ was the hot top-40 station with DJs like Lee Allen and Dave Prince. I got a night job in the news room pulling news stories off of the teletypes and giving them to the reporters. It was a junk job, but I was right in the area where the DJs worked; and to me, it was heaven.

I applied to Michigan State University, was accepted and joined the campus radio network where I soon found I could really do radio. This was the first time in my life I could do something effortlessly and still be better than most of my peers.

I left the University and began a ten year life that was very hard but exciting. After many jobs in small and lonely towns I got hired by chance at a new and exciting radio station that was using the FM band. Here, I joined four other young broadcasters and we developed the first free form commercial radio format. WABX became a sensation in Detroit and a programming leader nationally. I was the only one of this group of media pioneers to leave and eventually work at three of the other history-making early FM rock stations. They were KSAN in San Francisco, WMMR in Philadelphia, KLOS in Los Angeles, and the best one of them all—WNEW in New York City. There were other small moves here and there before all that and one of note was WKNR FM in Detroit.

I took part in the international practical joke called the "Paul is Dead" prank. "Paul" being Paul McCartney of the Beatles. Within three weeks of us starting our little joke it got out of hand until finally the reclusive Beatles had to step forward in front of television cameras and produce Paul McCartney.

I returned to the West Coast after New York and was hired by a production company owned by NBC Television and I wrote and produced segments for one of their crime shows and was the assistant to the producer. I returned to New York and did one of the first talk shows on the Internet during the great Internet boom (and scam, in my opinion). When that business crashed nation-wide, I was hired to be a programmer for Sirius Satellite in New York. I seem to have been first on quite a few pioneer adventures. I also was in charge of talent development at their New York studios.

Over the years I found myself in four or five books written about American media and, much to my surprise, found I was in the film documentary made in 2005 about the legendary rock band, the MC5. I was one of the early managers of the now infamous Grande Ballroom during the so called hippie days. I did the all night show on WLS FM in Chicago and watched every morning as the legendary rustic Paul Harvey taped his daily show.

Paul was a notorious right winger and hated the long haired youth movement of that time, but I found he seemed amused by my interest in his work. I was of course more than amused. I was overwhelmed by the ease and inventiveness of his unique style.

I am the announcer on the Bob Seger live album. It's funny; I have worked at radio stations and stood in the studio with fellow DJs while they played the album, and of course they had no interest in who the crazy-sounding mc was, and they never bothered to read the liner notes on the album. Saying nothing was more fun than bragging. I feel like I am doing that now, but in the interest of the reader that is the basic outline.

For this short piece I don't think it would be appropriate to drag out all the stories and events spent with crazy musicians and actors of world wide fame. Others have already done that. The way I lived my life is not a subject for this piece but I can tell you that the adventure took its toll. In fact, the life lived around the career was to me, now, the real interesting part.

Pam Coutilish (Scott)
CHS 1974
Director/Playwright/ Acting Teacher

In May 2009, classmate Diane Fraser Kirkbride, (CHS 1974) said when they were in school, Pam had always said she was going to New York and be on the stage.

Pam accomplished her goal.

February 2009, Bill Wentz, retired Clawson Middle School teacher, said Pam has lived in New York since 1979. She has a sister, Cindy Coutilish and a step-brother Jeff Gordon (CHS 1975) who is also in this book. The family lived at N. Washington and Broadacre. Wentz said that Pam changed her name to Pam Scott, 15 -20 years ago.

Here is what it says on The Creative Seed website: [1]

> Pamela Scott is a director, playwright, acting teacher and coach. Founder and Producing Artistic Director of Aching Dogs Theatre and most recently created Lunch: Live! a luncheon show for industry. Pamela teaches and directs at The Academy of Dramatic Arts and The School for Film and Television. Pamela graduated from Eastern Michigan University and The American Academy of Dramatic Arts. She studied with and assisted her mentor and friend, Sandra Seacat. Her classmates included, Jessica Lange, Brooke Shields, Betty Buckley, Gina Gershon, Don Johnson, and Marlo Thomas, and acting coaches Sheila Gray and Greta Seacat. Pamela has performed at

[1] www.thecreativeseed.com/keyin/index.htm

HERE, The Irish Arts Center, West Bank Downstairs Café/ Theatre, and Joseph Papp's Public Theatre.

Her 15 One-acts have been produced at numerous theaters in LA, FL and NYC. Her full-length play *The Unwrapping of Christmas* received the Alan Contini award for best new play from The Columbia University Dramatists and was produced at the Irish Arts Center. She is currently working on several screenplays and plays."

David Frezza

CHS 1969

Actor/Singer/Dancer

David Frezza grew up on the third block of Redruth. He was the son of Louis & Hazel Frezza. Siblings were Mary Ann (CHS 1971) and Paul (CHS 1974) Frezza.

In April 2009 Shirley Dittmar Wilson (CHS 1945) said she was a high school counselor in 1969, the time of the Class of 1969's Washington D.C. Senior trip. Once in Washington, there was a curfew put in place, as there were demonstrations going on for the anniversary of Martin Luther King's assassination. Everyone was confined to the motel. As a courtesy, the motel opened up a conference room and everyone from the motel could congregate there. Shirley remembers the girls played around doing ballerina moves. Dave joined them and really seemed to enjoy the dancing, and he was good.

May 2009 Dave Frezza wrote:

> I took dance lessons at Borgo Sisters School of Dance, just up the road from Dondero High School in Royal Oak, from the time I was nine years old.
>
> Tap, jazz, ballroom, disco, gymnastics and ethnic—I did them all. At Wayne State University after U of D, I took Modern Dance and joined a modern dance company for a short time.
>
> I loved going to the dances at school because not many guys danced and from my training and passionate interest in it, I could dance better than all of the guys and most of the girls. It got me a lot of attention. Most of it good, but some not so good. I had many girls interested in me be-

cause I could dance. I had many fights with guys who questioned my orientation because I was a dancer.

Dance made me a better athlete and I know that it greatly enhanced my baseball abilities. Dance develops a keen awareness in a person of exactly where there body is in space and helps with coordination, balance, agility and flexibility. I know I became a better baseball player because I combined all of those forces to become a fast ball pitcher.

I played varsity starting pitcher all four years at CHS. I was All-State Starting Pitcher in my Senior year and other state awards in my earlier years, but I don't have a record of the specific awards. Yes, I was drafted by the Montreal Expos (now "the Nats") in the 1969 June draft. I did not sign—probably my only real regret in life.

In the summer of 1969, I pitched the starting and closing games for the A&B Brokers in downtown Detroit to win the National Amateur Baseball Federation Class D (18u) Championship. We got our names engraved in gold lettering on a black bat that was submitted to the Baseball Hall of Fame. I had 25 strike-outs in 16 innings.

I had been working at the Borgo Sisters School of Dance teaching dance and gymnastics since I was 15 and had a girlfriend at Bishop Foley High School, so I did not want to accept the full scholarships offered to me by Arizona State, Western Michigan or any of the other notable schools. Instead I took a full ride guaranteed 4 year scholarship to the University of Detroit, majoring in Mathematics with a minor in Philosophy.

At the end of my junior year, I was selected to play in the Cape Cod League for the Harwich Mariners. The Cape Cod League was the premiere amateur baseball league for college players in the country. There were great numbers of pro scouts at almost every game. A large number of players signed pro contracts at the end of their summer playing there. The level of play was unlike anything I had experienced and it was a thrilling time for me all the way up to the point at which I permanently damaged my pitching arm. At this point in my life, I had been gunned at over 100 mph. I thought I was on my way to a big baseball career. A severe rotator cuff injury ended it for me. Back then they could not offer much to rectify the situation.

At the dance school, I helped increase the enrollment from 400 students per week when I started to 1800 students per week when I left at 25 years old. My greatest achievement was in making it OK for hundreds of boys in the local communities to learn to dance, giving them confidence on many levels. I choreographed musicals at CHS and other local high schools, including Birmingham Seaholm High School where I met Helen Wood, an Australian foreign exchange student. I ultimately left the States for Australia at the age of 25 to marry Helen in Sydney, Australia.

I got work the only way I could in Australia, which meant performing, since I did not have a legal visa or work permit. It's much easier to get work in the fast and loose field of performing than it is in the formal business world using a math degree as your greatest accomplishment. I joined several small time dance companies and paid my dues in what is a very small industry compared to the States. Within two years, I was doing variety shows on television supporting major Australian, English and occasionally American singers.

Because the industry is small there, it is almost imperative that you learn to sing and act to be able to work as many jobs as possible. In the end, I had done 11 movies working with Aussies Brian Brown, Jack Thompson, Julie Anthony, Rolfe Harris and my favorite—Paul Hogan in his first ever movie effort. I did several national television variety shows (one with Rolfe Harris of *Tie Me Kangaroo Down Sport*).

I did many plays and musicals, i.e. *The Rocky Horror Show, The Best Little Whorehouse in Texas, Guys and Dolls, Chicago,* etc. I guested with the Sydney Theatre Company for their production of *Chicago* for a year and a half, and we were invited to the Hong Kong Festival of the Arts as Australia's only representative in the two weeks leading up to the Chinese New Year in 1982.

I played Brad Majors, the all-american goodie-two-shoes boy, in *The Rocky Horror Show* for two years. We traveled and lived in all the major and some minor cities of Australia except Darwin. On that tour, we recorded six of the best songs from the show and that recording is still available for sale now.

I worked with some fairly big name artists over my ten years in Australia, including Robert Vaughan, James Coburn, Matt Dillon (I taught him to dance for the movie we did), Tony Randall, Chelsea Brown's night club act (formerly of *Laugh-In*), "The Two Ronnies" (English Comedians), Julie Anthony (now Dame, I believe), Elton John, etc.

I partied with Mel Gibson at an after show party. He came to see our version of Rocky and our cast and that of another across the street kept a Melbourne pub open till 5AM dancing, drinking and "carrying on" as they call it. Ladies, Mel is only about 5' 7" tall—not that size matters.

I played the Sydney Opera House in a four character original play called *The Conquest of Carmen Miranda* for close to a year. It was one of my favorite gigs, because I lived in Manly, a beach community in the northern beach suburbs on the other side of Sydney Harbor. Every day, I would take the ferry across arguably one of the most beautiful harbors in the world right up to the steps of the Opera House. I would meet world famous performers in the green room who were there for operas, symphonies, classical plays, etc. and have dinner with them. Then I would do my performance and take a late moonlight cruise back to my apartment at the beach. It seemed about as far from Detroit living as one could imagine.

I learned to SCUBA in Australia and would dive three to five times per week. Everywhere I traveled, with shows all up and down the Australian coast and the Indian Ocean off of Perth, I would engage local divers to set up dives to see the local hot spots. And yeah, there are a lot of sharks in those waters, but there are so many other beautiful creatures, especially up on the Great Barrier Reef.

I traveled and performed in New Zealand, Hong Kong, Macao, Singapore, Bangkok, Bali, and all over Australia.

I even got a chance to play baseball again. Australia was developing their own major league baseball program. I tried out for a team, don't remember our name at this point, but was selected as a starting pitcher and played baseball for two more years that I never thought would happen. The caliber of play was roughly equivalent to a good division 2 college program here in the States.

I am now in Bethesda, Maryland, having left my role as Executive Vice President of Sales, Marketing and Business

Development of a $76 Mil company to become a residential realtor and master of my own time and business. Having divorced my Aussie wife (not her fault), I am now married to a native Marylander and have one 22 year old step-son who is still going to school while working full time at Lockheed Martin and one 16 year old son I must claim as my own who is attending a private school 23 miles from here in Virginia. You see, my 16 year old Damon is a right-handed fastball pitcher throwing 92 mph as a sophomore. He was recruited by an excellent baseball school which not only won their conference championship this season, but also won their State Championship. So you may yet see a Frezza pitching for a major league baseball team. And guess what? His high school coach is a part time scout for the Detroit Tigers, so who knows . . .

I have very warm memories of my time in Clawson, especially the July 4th Parade, baseball at Clawson Park, the roller rink and the feeling of community in a simpler time. I have been back in the States now for 20 years. I had to sell the family home on Redruth recently because my dad died 10 years ago and my mom died a couple of years ago. It feels very sad to drive down the street and know that only the Hendricksons are left of the folks who lived there while I was growing up. I am sure though that the new blood will help to grow Clawson's tightly knit community into a warm, inviting hometown for lots of other adventurers, who will then go out into the rest of the states—or the world for that matter—to make their marks. And one day they will get a call out of the blue from Bill Hayes asking them to write something of their life's journey to share with the home town crowd.

Ken Gardestad
CHS 1966
Swedish Song Writer and Architect

Ken Gardestad was a Swedish foreign exchange student who lived with the Hugh and Wanda Hayes family for the 1965-66 school year. The Hayes children consisted of Bill (CHS 1963), Ray (CHS 1964), Dolores (CHS 1966), Don (CHS 1967) and Rhonda (CHS 1970) Hayes. They lived at 134 Redruth.

Ken wrote his biography below in June 2009.

I was born in 1948 and grew up in Sollentuna, a large suburb just six miles north of Stockholm, the capitol of Sweden. I was the second child in the family. Kjell, my older brother, was four years older than I. My mother Margit was at that time working as a secretary at Vattenfall, the Swedish national energy company. My father Arne was working for NK, the most famous department store in Stockholm. Sweden chose to be neutral during WWII and was spared from direct consequences of destruction, unlike most countries in Europe. The economic situation thus allowed for creating new political solutions. So, as a two year old child I entered a new social institution called "daghem"—the beginning of the modern daycare center, and free of charge. My mother took me there on her bike and picked me up when she arrived from her work almost ten hours later. The days were long, but I liked it anyway, even though I was eagerly waiting for my mother to show up.

At seven I started in the first grade. The class-room was located in the basement of an apartment house due to the baby-boom after the war. I spent my second and third year in the same house I was living in. I remember that I wanted to impress my class-mates, so during a break I ran to my apartment, put on a record with Paul Anka, opened the window and let them listen to ”Diana”.

In 1956, when I was eight, my brother Ted was born. I became his protégé the day my mother brought him home to our apartment. The hall was dark but his appearance lit up the space.

A few years later we were engaged in making music. Ted was six and he wanted an accordion. He started immediately to compose. I used my mother's guitar, mostly to find a way to impress girls.

I was quite successful in school. I got good grades by working hard and I was also good in sports. I was chosen the best athlete in Sollentuna at the end of my ninth grade, 1964. So, I applied for an American Field Service scholarship. My father helped me out to write the application.

I left Sweden for USA in August 1965. I was amazed by the sky-scrapers in New York, my stop-over before flying to Detroit and Clawson. I was picked up at the Metro airport by my new family, The Hayes. It was the beginning of fall but the air was still warm and humid. The electrical billboard of Goodyear was ticking the numbers of tires sold to the market. Peaches were growing. They wondered who I was. Was I good in sports? I weighed 125 pounds and was maybe 5 feet 7 inches tall. And the Hayes were big. I grew up during that senior year. I played in the junior basketball team, but I was more successful as a half mile runner. I ended up as number five in the last conference meet. I cried; I wanted to be number one.

When I got back in August 1966 my brother Ted had participated in a major production for the Swedish Television. I had changed, but the family liked the old Ken better. I had become too independent.

In 1968, an American movie production company called us and wondered if Ted could come to an audition. They had heard that he could play the accordion and they wanted him to try out for a role in the movie. I carried his accordion and after two meetings they wanted me to be part of the movie too, as I was there anyway. It was a grand production with several Swedish well-known actors, but also the American star Robert Stack, known for his TV series.

The film was called *A Story of a Woman*, and the leading female role was played by Bibbi Andersson, one of the favourite actresses of the world-renowned Swedish director Ingmar Bergman. Maybe the movie wasn´t the best in the world, but we enjoyed it; and it allowed us to buy new equipment for our small studio.

The year after, 1969, I visited Clawson and found America struck by the Vietnam War. Everybody was feeling bad and I had been turned down by a girlfriend again, two reasons to write a song. I presented the song to Ted when I got back. That song gradually changed our lives.

It wasn´t all music. In 1968, during the student revolution, I was emitted to the Royal Institute of Technology in Stockholm in order to study to become an architect. I was also involved in sports and took my interest for basketball to a new level. Eventually, eight years later in 1976, my team, Tureberg, won our conference and tried out for the major league. I was the point guard of the starting line.

I also carried my brother Ted´s tennis rackets to his tournaments. I cheered him on when he played against the best players in his age. At fifteen, in 1971, Ted had become the second best player in Sweden, only surpassed by Björn Borg.

At the same time we had enough musical material to try to get a contract with any Record company around. We walked a half mile across one of the major parks in Stockholm to a record company we vaguely recognized. One week later we had signed a deal with Polar Music. The year after, in 1972, we had sold more albums than any previous act in Sweden.

The song that took us to the number one position on the chart was the song I presented to Ted in 1969. He had altered it to the better and the song "Jag vill ha en egen måne" - "I Want a Moon of My Own" is now in 2009, one of our many songs everybody sings along to.

Our producers were Björn and Benny, the first half of ABBA, the second half, Annifrid and Agneta, were our choir. They participated on our first four albums, which all went Gold or better in 1972-1976.

In 1977 we flew to Los Angeles. We checked in at The Sunset Marquise at Sunset Boulevard, Hollywood. We had booked The Sound Labs Studio for our American album.

Our producer, Eiric Wangberg, had worked as a technical engineer on Paul McCartney's album *Ram* and was also involved in Diana Ross' album *Mahogony*, so he was all Ted and I wanted. When we were done we had been backed up by the group Toto, and both Dr John and John Mayall had participated. They sung the chorus on one of our songs, "Just For the Money." Maybe money was their motive, or maybe . . . they liked it?

Ted had an enormous ability to write music and he had a distinct high-pitched voice and an attractive look. I added the words to his melodies .We became a team that made music and words mix in a complete experience that still attracts many people.

During the 1980s we took a break from music. Ted wanted to explore his soul and I wanted to extend my skill in architecture. As a matter of fact, at the same time that I was involved in the music scene in USA in the later years of the 1970s I was working in Nigeria to design the new university in Port Harcourt. My design was the first building erected. I used that experience to apply for a Fulbright scholarship. In 1984 I moved to Boston to attend MIT. When I got back after two years and a Master of Science degree, I was for five years involved in designing offices with sky lit atriums.

The first years of the 1990s were hard for everybody. Nothing was built and many people were unemployed. I was lucky. I had time to write music, or as my skill was, to write the words to my brother's music. Ted and I could once again work closely together; however, the happy days were over. Ted had been struck by mental illness, something he vigorously denied. We recorded our last album in 1994, and once again we were number one on the charts.

In 1995 I was employed by the architectural firm Michelsen Architects. My job there was to design, as the architect in charge, new extensions to the airport of Stockholm, Arlanda. When I was done our design for the Air Traffic Control Center had won the price for the best Building in Sweden for the year 2000.

During the same period, 1997, I won a competition for designing "the school of the future—a school without references." That school in Flen in the middle of Sweden was inaugurated by our Swedish king in 1998.

My solutions to new ways of organizing educational spaces got me another job. After many discussions I was convinced to join a new organization called "Kunskapsskolan." Their aim was to become the best alternative to public schools and my design fitted their purpose. In Sweden every student can choose what school he or she wants to go to, public or private. The economy is taken care of by a voucher system that follows each student. One of my schemes, Kunskapsskolan in Nyköping, was given an award for best Architecture in that region in 2003.

The way of organizing spaces in accordance with pedagogical ideas has caught public attention in Great Britain. I´ve been a host to several study-groups from people around the world: Japan, Australia, USA, Holland, Germany, England, and I´ve been giving speeches on that topic in London, Manchester and Glasgow.

My brother Ted took his life in 1997. His mental illness brought him down. He never admitted to himself that he had any disease. He could not see himself in that situation. He fought for more than ten years to deny that he was ill. One day he gave way. He took his life.

The day he died people from newspapers and the Swedish television were standing at our doorstep, wondering about me and my family's reaction. At that moment I decided to tell our story and also to try to do something about it. Some of my best friends and I decided to start a fund for young people who cared for music. We wanted to bring hope and excitement and a will to enjoy the next day. The fund is called "Ted Gärdestad Minnesfond" equivalent to "Ted Gardestad Memory Fund." It gives awards to persons younger than 25 who win competitions writing music: any style, but with a heart—and with Swedish lyrics. This year we're celebrating this occasion for the tenth time.

I have written a book about Ted's life in the light of my perspective. I´ve pledged to try to get rid of the guilt and shame that haunts both the affected and their families. I´ve spent the last four years giving speeches to move the public awareness in that direction. My last speech a few weeks ago was held in front of a sold out crowd of 850 people in the Culture house in the northern town of Luleå.

Ted is dead but our music lives on. Last year there were 26 sold out concerts throughout Sweden. Our songs were performed by some of the best artists in Sweden. This year, 2009, the theme for the Stockholm Cultural Festival will be held in the name of our music. Our albums will once again be released but now in a complete CD-box, accompanied by TV-commercials and more concerts.

Christina Kokubo

CHS 1968

Movie and TV actress

Christina Kokubo was the daughter of Ted and Edythe Kokubo. Ted was on the Clawson School Board in the late 1960s and early 1970s. Christina has two siblings, Jared and John Kokubo. The Kokubos s moved to Birmingham from Clawson, so Jared and John may have graduated from a Birmingham School.

Chris went to Hollywood and became a movie and TV actress from the mid 1970s through the late 1980s. Her film credits include the movie *Midway* where she played Miss Haruko Sakura, the love interest of Ensign Garth, played by Edward Albert. Lead actors in the movie include Charlton Heston, Henry Fonda and Robert Wagner.

Chris was also in the movie *Yakuza* staring Robert Mitchum.

Her TV credits include *L.A. Law*; *Dying Time*; 13 episodes of *St. Elsewhere*; *Just between Friends*; *Hawaii Five-O* and *The Blue Knight*.

Janice Satow (CHS 1965) wrote the following, which she learned from a family friend, Sam Yanari, that knew the Kokubos.

> Christina wanted to do ballet but was too small. She was a very warm and generous person. She never married, but did date an actor from *Little House on the Prairie* (Yanari thought the person's name was John—or something like that. However the cast list does not include a John who could be the correct one.) She would come to Michigan occasionally and stay with John (her brother).
>
> She started an acting company in LA for handicapped and socially withdrawn people. I don't know the name or even if it still exists. Sam said a couple of years ago she was

diagnosed with breast cancer and one day the emails just stopped. He thinks she may have passed away.

Virginia "Ginger" Newman (CHS 1968) says Christina died of cancer December 2007. They were good friends in school.

Robert McKee

CHS 1959

Broadway Actor/ Screenwriter/Lecturer

The October 20, 2003 edition of *The New Yorker* contains an article titled “The Real McKee” by Ian Parker. He writes:

> ...McKee grew up in Clawson, a northern suburb of Detroit; his father was an engineer at General Motors and his mother worked in real estate. ‘My father was in many ways a marvelous guy,’ McKee told me. ‘He got me into reading. He had high standards. But he was also a paranoid alcoholic.’ McKee was sixteen when his father left the family... McKee had two younger brothers. One died in middle age; the other became a senior Ford executive, and has now retired and lives in Florida.
>
> McKee was a golf caddie from the age of twelve, and he won an Evans scholarship (given to caddies) to the University of Michigan. He had liked the idea of a career in dentistry, because of the free time for golfing it seemed to promise, but, after being given a part in a student play, he decided to major in English. He took a Master’s in theatre, and was taught by the late Kenneth Rowe, who had also taught Arthur Miller. McKee became a theater actor and a director, first in Michigan, then in London, and then, in the late sixties, in New York....”

Wikipedia, Internet encyclopedia, contains the following:

> Robert McKee, born 1941, is a creative writing instructor who is widely known for his popular "Story Seminar," which he developed when he was a professor at the University of Southern California. McKee is the author of a "screenwriters' bible" called *Story: Substance, Structure, Style* and the *Principles of Screenwriting*. Many of Holly-

wood's active screenwriters claim him as an inspiration. Rather than simply handling "mechanical" aspects of fiction technique such as plot or dialogue taken individually, McKee examines the narrative structure of a work and what makes the story compelling or not. This could work equally as well as an analysis of any other genre or form of narrative, whether in screenplay or any other form, and could also encompass nonfiction works as long as they attempt to "tell a story."

Early life in the theater:

Robert McKee began his theater career at the age of 9, playing the title role in a community theater production of *Martin the Shoemaker*. He continued acting as a teenager in theater productions in his hometown of Detroit, Michigan. Upon receiving the Evans scholarship, he attended the University of Michigan and earned a Bachelor's degree in English Literature. While an undergraduate, he acted in and directed over thirty productions. McKee's creative writing professor was the noted Kenneth Thorpe Rowe.

After completing his Bachelor of Arts degree, McKee toured with the APA (Association of Producing Artists) Repertory Company, appearing on Broadway alongside Helen Hayes, Rosemary Harris and Will Geer. He then received the Professional Theater Fellowship and returned to Ann Arbor, Michigan to earn his Master's degree in Theater Arts.

Upon graduating, McKee directed the Toledo Repertory Company, acted with the American Drama Festival, and became Artistic Director of the Aaron Deroy Theater. From there he traveled to London to accept the position of Artist-in-Residence at the National Theater where he studied Shakespearean production at the Old Vic theater. He then returned to New York and spent the next seven years as an actor/director in Broadway.

Mid-life in the film industry:

After deciding to move his career to film, McKee attended Cinema School at the University of Michigan. While there, he directed two short films: *A Day Off*, which he also wrote, and *Talk To Me Like The Rain*, adapted from a one-act play by Tennessee Williams. These two films won the Cine Eagle Award, awards at the Brussels and Grenoble

Film Festivals, and various prizes at the Delta, Rochester, Chicago, and Baltimore Film Festivals.

In 1979, McKee moved to Los Angeles, where he began to write screenplays and work as a story analyst for United Artists and NBC. He sold his first screenplay, *Dead Files,* to AVCO/Embassy Films, after which he joined the WGA (Writers Guild of America). His next screenplay, *Hard Knocks*, won the National Screenwriting Contest; since then McKee has had eight feature film screenplays purchased or optioned, including the feature film script *Trophy* for Warner Bros. (The film, however, was not produced). In addition to his screenplays, McKee has had a number of scripts produced for such television series as *Quincy, M.D.* (starring Jack Klugman), *Columbo* (starring Peter Falk), *Spenser: for Hire,* and *Kojak* (starring Telly Savalas).

Starting the STORY seminar

In 1983, as Fulbright Scholar, McKee joined the faculty of the School of Cinema-Television at the University of Southern California (USC), where he began offering his famous STORY Seminar class. A year later, McKee opened the course to the public, giving a 3-day, 30-hour intensive class to sold-out audiences around the world.

Since 1984, more than 50,000 students have taken McKee's course, at various cities around the world: Los Angeles, New York, London, Paris, Sydney, Toronto, Boston, Las Vegas, San Francisco, Helsinki, Oslo, Munich, Tel Aviv, Singapore, Barcelona and more.

Current life and awards:

Robert McKee is among the most widely known screenwriting lecturers. According to his web site, McKee's former students include 26 Academy Award winners, 125 Emmy Award winners, 19 WGA (Writers Guild of America) Award winners and 16 DGA (Directors Guild of America) Award winners (all participated in McKee's course before or after winning their award; not all were awarded for writing). He was profiled by Bob Simon of *60 Minutes* for CBS news, and CNN recently did a profile and review of McKee and the Story Seminar. The actors Kirk Douglas and John Cleese have taken his seminar.

McKee continues to be a project consultant to major film and television production companies, as well as to major software firms (Microsoft, etc.) and television news departments. In addition, several companies such as ABC, Disney, Miramax, PBS, Nickelodeon and Paramount regularly send their entire creative and writing staffs to his lectures.

In 2000, McKee won the International Moving Image Book Award for his book *Story* (Regan Books/Haper Collins). The book, currently in its 19th printing in the United States and its 14th printing in the UK, has become required reading for film and cinema schools at Harvard, Yale, UCLA, USC and Tulane universities. The book was on the Los Angeles Times best-seller list for 20 weeks.

McKee's other credits include writing and presenting the BBC series Filmworks, the Channel Four series 'Reel Secrets', the BAFTA Award-winning *J'Accuse Citizen Kane* television program which he wrote and hosted, and the writing of *Abraham*, the four-hour mini-series on Turner Network Television (TNT) which starred Richard Harris, Barbara Hershey and Maximilian Schell.

Jason Mulheisen
CHS 1990
Movie and TV Actor

Jason Mulheisen is the son of John and Sandy Mulheisen. Jason has a sister Amy (CHS 1994) Mulheisen. They grew up on Kinross. He was a very good basketball player in high school. His mother said Jason went off to Albion College, Oakland University and Wayne State University, graduating in 1995.

In September 1995 Jason left for California to try and become an actor. He joined the Screen Actors Guild and said he would give it 10 years to work out and if it didn't he would come home. Jason became an "extra" in various movies and TV shows. He was on *Friends* and *Seinfield* and had a speaking part as a reporter in the made for TV movie *Three Secrets* (1999). After ten years Jason moved back home, got married, has two children, and lives in Troy, Michigan. He is a realtor in the Clawson/Troy area. He also does modeling for auto shows and clothes. He has done Big Boy and Honda commercials for TV and has made various teaching type videos for companies.

On May 31, 2009, Sandy Mulheisen advised me that Jason had just done a Keno TV commercial, a couple weeks ago, for the Michigan State Lottery Commission at the Tavern On The Main (old Main Inn) on S. Main in Clawson.

> I listed some facts for you about me. Might not be a formal, proper bio, but feel free to word it however you like. My acting career in LA was honestly not much to write home about. I did have a few lines in a couple TV movies and a couple of soap operas, but nothing major. Worked as an extra for a year on a bunch of shows. I've had more success after I moved back to Michigan.
>
> Born Feb 16, 1972—Lived in Clawson on Kinross from 1975 until 1995.—Sister Amy, '95 grad.—Attended Baker,

Schalm, Clawson Middle School, and Clawson High School, class of '90.—Played 3 years varsity Baseball and 3 years varsity Basketball in High School. All Area in basketball a few times.—Lived in Los Angeles from 1995-2005—Appeared in TV movie *Three Secrets* and few episodes of *Days of our Lives*—Since moving back to Michigan, I've appeared in two commercials and over 20 industrial films ranging from the Big Three to the US Customs Dept.—Currently live in Troy—Wife Elizabeth, son Trevor, daughter Claire.

I have always loved my time in Clawson. I had a great time growing up there. After living in another state for 10 years, meeting new people, having a job where I work closely with people all over the country, I found that it was a unique place to grow up. I am still friendly and in contact with well over 50 people that I grew up with, in one class or another. This is a rarity, I assure you. People are often surprised by this.

Daniel Scanlon
CHS 1994
Illustrator/Cartoonist/ Movie Animator

Dan Scanlon is the son of Betty Scanlon Zych. Dan attended Schalm School, Clawson Middle School and Clawson High.

The Fall 2005 edition of REEL NEWS contains the following about Dan:

> Dan Scanlon is living his dream. From the time he attended elementary school in Clawson he wanted to make movies. His first film (*The Fwebicks*) was made when he was only 9 years old.
>
> He kept focused throughout his high school career and made a Best of Show animation (*Andy*) at the MSFVF while attending the William D. Ford Career Tech Center in Westland. He is also a charter member of the Student Animation Workshop (SAW).
>
> After graduating in 1994, he attended the Columbus School of Art (Columbus, Ohio) on a scholarship where he majored in animation. In 1998, he started his first job with an animation company in Columbus called Character Builders where he worked on Disney sequels (*Little Mermaid 2* and *101 Dalmatians 2*).
>
> In 2001, Dan headed west to California and landed a job at Pixas. He is a storyboard artist for director John Lassiter and is currently working on a new feature animation called *Cars*.
>
> Working on a big feature film is keeping Dan pretty busy. He said that they will have drawn more than 40,000

storyboard panels for *Cars* before it's completed. At 28 years old, Dan is still living his dream.

In July 2009 the *Royal Oak Review*, a free newspaper that covers Royal Oak and Clawson, had a article on Dan Scanlon.

Over the last 6 years he wrote, produced and acted in a independent full length live-action movie named *Tracy*. It was filmed in San Francisco and Clawson; and recently had a special screening at the Main Art Theatre. He still works for Pixar and was a story-board artist for "Cars" and the upcoming *Toy Story 3*. *Tracy* was also shown in the Detroit-Windsor Film Festival.

You can see a trailer of the movie at www.tracymovie.com, which contains more information about Dan and the people with whom he works.

Angeline Squires
CHS 1933
International Dancing Star

Angeline Squires was born in 1915. She was the granddaughter of Stephen and Kittie Squires of 285 Massoit. According to Bris Hunter (CHS 1943) Angeline was the daughter of Bert Squires. Bert was never married. He hung out at the Main Inn (present day Tavern On the Main). Bert had a brother, Fred Squires, who also lived with Stephen and Kittie. Bris said that Fred had joined the Canadian Army in WWI and half his face was blown off in the battle at Vimy Ridge in France. The doctors had put a silver plate on Fred's head and he was never quite right after that. Fred hung out at Ted's Bar, at Jefferson and Main Street. The 1920 census shows Stephen, Kittie, Fred and Angeline Squires all living in the Royal Oak Park Subdivision, Royal Oak Township. 285 Massoit would be in this subdivision.

Deloris Kumler, retired curator of the Clawson Historical Museum, said that Angeline didn't graduate from high school. She left school early and ran away from home because of poor home conditions. She became a dancer on a ship.

A newspaper article, from unknown source, with picture, from about 1938, can be seen at the museum. The article reads:

Dancer Home After Two Years in Europe

> Home for the first time after more than two years abroad, Southern Oakland county's most famous dancer, Miss Angeline of Clawson, is expecting to leave 'any day now' for further engagements in New York and Chicago with her partner, Berinoff. She danced before royalty in Europe, returned home to visit her grandparents, Mr. And Mrs. Stephen Squires, 285 Massoit Avenue, Clawson.

Leaving for Europe in May, 1935, Miss Angeline danced before the King and Queen of Denmark, the King of Sweden, King Carol of Rumania and the Duke of Windsor before he renounced his English crown. She also did her ballroom and acrobatic dancing before Wallis Simpson at the famous French summer resort, Cannes, on the Riviera. That was before Mrs. Simpson was married to the Duke.

When she was 10 years old, Angeline began studying her art under Dorothy Funk Miller, who has conducted dancing classes here for a number of years. The Clawson girl realized the dreams of every young dancer after further study in Detroit and New York. Her first contract was with a road show, which she left Clawson High School to join. Since then she has also danced in operas, musical comedies and has done concert work.

Despite being busy most of the time, Angleine found time in Europe to become slightly homesick. She accordingly sent for her sister, Alberta, whose home also is in Clawson. Alberta arrived in England in time to help Angeline celebrate her twenty-third birthday anniversary on Oct. 29. The younger sister is returning to her grandparents' home from England this month.

Angeline's hobbies (her work is really her hobby) include the collecting of photographs, cards, money and dolls in foreign lands. Her dolls comprise her favorite collection. She has about 25, purchased in different countries and dressed in native costume.

How she keeps at her regular weight of 96 to 99 pounds is revealed in the fact that Angeline gets in an hour of practice daily while working two shows a day. She also watches her diet closely, confining her choices of foods to salads, spinach, rare steak or rare calf liver.

Her favorite foreign food is found in Italy. It is 'very tasty, the way they season it.' In the United States, she likes to patronize the American-Chinese restaurants and then, of course, her grandmother's offerings also are first rate.

Additional facts about the Clawson girl include: She is five feet in height, is of French and English origin, says Catherine is her middle name, has danced with Berinoff more than three years, and declares she does not intend to go to Hollywood, although she admits the film companies and their salary checks might cause a change of mind. Her last name, of course, is Squires.

Another newspaper article, *The Daily Tribune*, Royal Oak, dated August 15, 1947, with picture, can also be found at the museum. The article reads:

Clawson Dancer Keeps Interest in Dolls

Whenever she has an opportunity to return to her Clawson home, over 200 dolls from every corner and capital of Europe remind Angeline Wynters of travels on the way to her present success as a romantic dancer.

Angeline, the feminine half of the dance team 'Wynters and Angeline', now headlining the floor show at the Northwood Inn, is the former Angeline Squires who left Clawson to become a top dancer.

She and Allen Wynter, her husband and partner, maintain a home at 830 North Main street, but Angeline's dolls really belong to her grandmother, Mrs. Stephen Squires, 285 Massoit avenue, who raised Angeline and started her on her career.

When Angeline took a four year tour of Europe before the war, she sent dolls from every city and country to Mrs. Squires as souvenirs of performances before royalty and success in Europe's greatest cities.

Each doll is dressed in a costume of its native country. There are dolls from Hungary, Rumania, Austria, Italy, Egypt, Greece, France, Denmark, Belgium, Sweden, Norway, and Great Britain.

There is an Egyptian doll with a long veil hanging from its face. Dolls acquired in Greece . . . wear short skirts and boots common among Grecian peasantry. There are dolls in soldiers' uniforms, dolls in fancy dress, and dolls in the national counterpart of every day garb.

The costumes are all handmade and were selected because they represent some type of clothing in vogue at the time Angeline acquired them. The collection is valuable as an example of authentic costuming. For that reason it eventually may be loaned to a museum where it will be available for inspection and study of students of costume.

Angeline, then Angeline Squires, met Allen Wynters in Hollywood where he was a dancing coach and she had an

engagement doing solo dancing. They danced together……"
(end of newspaper clipping)

Bris Hunter says that when Angeline retired she wanted to stay in Michigan. Her husband, Allen Wynters wanted to move to California. They parted company and each went their own way. Bris said Angeline was part Chippewa Indian and she is buried on Mackinac Island.

Terri Turner

CHS 1986

Miss Michigan Teen USA 1986

Terri Turner is the daughter of Frank and Linda Turner. They lived on N. Marias in Clawson. Terri is the youngest of three children. Her two older brothers are Frank (CHS 1980) and Daniel (CHS 1983) Turner. Terri married Andy Helmuth (CHS 1985). Andy was drafted by the Chicago Blackhawks in 1985. Terri was Miss Michigan Teen USA in 1986 and competed in the national contest.

I remember the whole town watching the national contest on TV. No matter how much we rooted for her, she didn't win. nevertheless, it was exciting to watch her on TV.

Al Terwilliger

Actor/Singer/Dancer/ Inventor

Al Terwilliger was born in 1939 in Clawson, Michigan. He was the son of Durward "Pat" and Lenor "Mickey" Terwilliger. The Terwilligers owned Twig's Restaurant, southeast corner of 14 Mile & Main, in the early 1940s. Al went to kindergarten in Clawson.

The family moved to Claire, Michigan where Al finished his schooling and graduated from Claire High School in 1957. In the early 1970s Al and his wife, Myra, moved on to Massoit Street in Clawson and have lived in Clawson since then. They raised two daughters, Taryn and Melissa Terwilliger, in Clawson. The girls attended Our Shepherd Lutheran School in Birmingham and then Southfield Christian High School where they graduated.

The following is from *Hoof Beats Magazine*, March 2005:

> You might think Al Terwilliger was born to be a lot of things—and you would be right. But Terwilliger is first and foremost an inventor, and don't ever think otherwise....
>
> Al Terwilliger is the brains, the hands and the face behind Protecto Horse Equipment Inc., one of harness racing's most respected and accomplished equipment manufacturers...... He is known, quite simply, as the Protecto Man...
>
> ...The name on the flyer is Al Terry. The image is a dark-suited young man, a charming smile on his lips and a twinkle in his eye. His microphone is poised, ready to carry his next song to audiences far and wide.

It barely takes a blink before the facial similarities appear. Al Terry is Al Terwilliger.

But this is no flash-in-the pan publicity shot. Terwilliger started performing as a pre-teen on *Ted Mack's Original Amateur Hour*, an on-air talent show that appeared on all four major networks during its incredible run from 1948 to 1970.

A graduate of the Detroit Conservatory of Music, he went on to study at the Julliard School of Music and become an honest-to-goodness performer on the stage and television...

...During his youth spent with his family in the racing business, Terwilliger was introduced to comedic actor Andy Devine, known for his distinctive two-tone voice in such films as *The Spirit of Notre Dame*, and on television in *Adventures of Wild Bill Hickok* and the children's show *Andy's Gang*.

Terwilliger used to help Devine pick winners at the races, and was handed his own winning ticket when Devine recommended the budding thespian for a role in the Broadway show *Never Too Late*.

Terwilliger went on to serve as understudy to the noted actor Robert Morse during the highly successful Broadway run of *How to Succeed in Business Without Really Trying,* the story of J. Pierpont Finch's unlikely rise up the corporate ladder.

I sat there in that theater and never got called on," Terwilliger said with a shake of his head. "Bobby Morse never would miss a performance. I'd say, 'Jeeze, break a leg or do some damn thing!'

He roomed with another Michigan native during those early years, a struggling actor named George Peppard, who was driving a cab while awaiting his big break...

...'One day I woke up in a hotel room, and I didn't know where I was,' he recalled. 'It scared me a little. People think in show business you have a lot of friends but you don't. It's a lonesome life. You have a lot of acquaintances.'

Terwilliger has acted with Dan Dailey in the play *Anniversary Waltz*, with Andy Devin and Vivian Blaine in *Never Too Late*. He has also worked with Ann Southern, Walter Brennan and many other great stars.

From a *Daily Tribune* article dated January 6, 1993:

Kentucky comes to Clawson

A Clawson man is now a Kentucky colonel. That honorary title was bestowed on Al Terwilliger, 53, who sports a colorful life, especially in the sport of horse racing.

He also met an obscure actor, Ronald Reagan, who later helped in Terwilliger's campaign for the position of lieutenant Governor of Michigan.

Although Terwilliger was defeated for political office, he went on to gain fame in harness racing with his safety devices for horse and rider.

Terwilliger ran for lieutenant Governor in Michigan in the 1974 election. Eldon K. Andrews was running for Governor on the Conservative Party ticket. They were defeated.

Victoria Rose Zalewski

CHS 2000

Puppet Fabricator

Victoria Rose Zalewski is the daughter of James and Karla Zalewski. Victoria has at least one sibling, Karen. They live on Massoit.

Victoria whose professional name is "Victoria Rose" is a puppet fabricator.

In the February 18, 2009 edition of the *Royal Oak Daily Tribune*, is the following article by Catherine Kavanaugh:

> Victoria Zalewski is placing her order for a Detroit Zoo snow globe with the memorabilia she collected while working on *Coraline*, the longest stop-action film made to date.
>
> The 26-year-old Clawson resident had several behind-the-scenes roles in the 3-D adventure about a young girl (voice by Dakota Fanning) who moves from Michigan to Oregon and discovers a secret door in her home.
>
> The door leads to a fantasy world Zalewski helped create as a model maker, silicone caster and seamer. She had a hand in crafting the talking cat that befriends Coraline, 500 Scottie dogs and a thousand miscellaneous hands, boots and tongues.
>
> It was a dream job for the former student, wooed mid-term from her animation and puppet fabrication classes at the Center of Creative Studies by Laika Entertainment.

I thought it would take me five years to get hired there," said Zalewski, a CCS graduate who first learned about mold making from her father, James.

He got choked up at the premiere earlier this month when he saw the name of his daughter, who usually goes by her middle name Victoria Rose, in the movie credits.

My dad totally cried because I used my last name out of respect for him," Zalewski said. "He was my biggest inspiration. When I was 8, we watched *Alien* frame by frame and he pointed out all the animatronics.

For *Coraline*, Zalewski helped assemble tiny puppets—the hand-made star is 8 inches tall—and remove the visible seams after the molds were cast and cured. She also built up a supply of foam latex legs and tails for the feline character as well as hands the size of her thumbnail for Coraline.

The hands were really delicate so they would break easily," Zalewski said. "In production we would go through 30-40 a week.

In a stop-motion film, puppets move one frame at a time. The *Coraline* crew, which included "old school talent" affiliated with *Star Wars*, didn't use any computer-generated graphics.

Everything you see is a tangible object," Zalewski said. "The rain on the window is hot glue. All 500 seats in the theater had a functioning dog sitting in it. Everything was made as close to reality as possible. It was amazing to work on."

Zalewski returned home from production work with one of the keys Coraline uses to open the secret door, a glass-encased mouse given as presents to the crew, and a limited-edition pair of Nike dunks Coraline wears. However, she wasn't lucky enough to land one of the snow globes that remind Coraline of her happier days in Michigan.

She also wants to have a career in the film industry, taking off in Michigan because of state tax incentives.

...Karla Zalewski said *Coraline* kept her daughter busy at Laika, which is based in Portland, Ore., from January 2007 through September 2008. However, she expects her daughter's talents will take her far professionally and geographically.

"She has always been such a goal-oriented person," Karla Zalewski said. "She once did a paper on (*Coraline* director) Henry Selick and she told me, 'One day I'll work for him.'

"She is an example that it doesn't matter where you come from. If you work hard and believe in yourself you can do it."

BUSINESS

	**Robert Birch** **CHS 1963** **Industrial Developer**

Alex and Beatrice Birch moved to Clawson in 1937. Bob was the youngest of four boys. Alex (CHS 1955) became an Anesthesiologist; Charles (CHS 1958) became a high school teacher in Durand, Michigan; and Jerry (CHS 1961) became a Department Manager of graphics and computer technology for Washington Public Power in central Washington. Bob married Annette Sawicki (CHS 1964).

After graduating from Clawson High School in 1963, Bob went on to attend Western Michigan University and obtained a BS degree in Industrial Engineering in 1967. After graduation he began his 14-year career at General Motors where he held positions in Engineering, Quality Control and Production. During this time he was instrumental in launching two new General Motors automotive plants, one on the east side and one on the west side of Pontiac, Michigan.

In 1976 Bob received a "Successful Graduate of the Year" award from Western Michigan University. Years later, in 2008, Bob received the "Excellence in Professional Accomplishments" award, also from Western Michigan University.

In 1981, he accepted a position with Nissan Motor Manufacturing to set up the quality control activities for their new 3.2 million square foot U.S. manufacturing facility in Smyrna, Tennessee. The Japanese understood that their quality systems could not be lifted from Japan and placed in the United States because of the cultural differences. It was Bob's responsibility to analyze the Japanese quality systems and develop a "blend" of American/Japanese systems that would be workable in the United States.

During his 13 years with Nissan, Bob held positions in Quality Control, Purchasing, and Supplier Development where he studied and implemented Japanese manufacturing and purchasing philosophies within the plant and at the U.S. part suppliers.

In 1994, Bob accepted the position of Vice President of Purchasing and Logistics for Mercedes-Benz U.S. International, Inc., located in Tuscaloosa, Alabama. He was responsible for Production Part Purchasing, Indirect Material Purchasing, Production Control, Inventory Control and Forward Planning for the Mercedes Assembly plant that produces three Mercedes car lines. Bob maintained a residence in Stuttgart Germany as well as the United States for the first three years of employment as he was required to spend a large amount of his time in both locations.

The original plant was designed to produce Mercedes SUVs for worldwide sales, but sales of the M-Class were so great the plant could only produce enough vehicles for the costumers in the United States. For this reason, Bob contracted a facility in Austria to produce the M-Class for Europe sales and set up a part collection and distribution center in the United States to export U.S. built "kits of parts" to that facility.

Bob retired from Mercedes in 2001.

When asked "What was it like growing up in Clawson?", Bob responded as follows:

> In the late 1920s there was a house with a two car detached garage located on the southeast corner of the current Bywood and Phillips Ave. The house burned down so the owners converted the detached garage into a small house. In 1937 my parents, Alex and Bea Birch, purchased the garage house and moved in. It was there that my three brothers and I were raised until 1954 when we purchased a new house located up the street at 915 Phillips Ave.
>
> I remember Clawson in the late 1940s and early 1950s as being very rural. There were houses on the west end of Phillips Ave and on Selfridge with huge fields behind them. Mushrooms and wild strawberries grew in those fields and we picked them during the season. The wild strawberries were sweet and juicy but each strawberry was only about 1/4 of an inch in diameter. My parents paid me 5 cents per quart to pick wild strawberries, but they were so small and hidden in the weeds, it took me most of a day to gather just one quart.

In the early years of my life, Clawson had *spirit*. We had so many free (or very cheap) activities for kids I was always busy. I went to Day Camp at the park in the summer, played in little league baseball, was in the 4th of July kiddy parade each year and later on played in band and engaged in school sporting activities. I also was a member of a Boy Scout troop that met in the Junior High gym once a week.

In the summers we played outside from 'morning till dusk' and in the process, life long friendships developed between neighborhood kids. The cold winters didn't keep us inside either. We'd bundle up, go outside and make snowmen and snow forts, and of course a snowball fight would always ensue.

The city made several ice skating rinks around town and they were free for anyone that wanted to use them. As children, our lives were very different from staying indoors and sitting in front of a computer for entertainment as so many kids do today.

Of all the activities offered in Clawson, I liked the 4th of July the best. The parade, the games at the park, the music, the bands, beauty contest, the gathering of relatives and friends, and of course, the fireworks.

We as children were given a wonderful life growing up in Clawson in the late 1940s and 1950s. We were given a unique opportunity to engage in healthy entertainment because of the many volunteers that took on the responsibility of organizing these activities for us. It was these people that created 'the spirit of Clawson.'

William Morean
CHS 1973
Co-owner of
Jabil Circuits

Bill Morean was the son of William E. and Audry Morean. Bill's sister was Beth Ann (CHS 1971) Morean. The 1960 Polk's Directory, found at the Clawson Historical Museum, said Mr. Morean owned Bill's Trenching Service at 345 S.Crooks Road.

According to Wayne Neff (CHS 1962), retired Clawson Postman, the Moreans lived at 317 S. Crooks. Wayne said the Moreans moved the next street over to 345 S. Batchewana. Wayne was aware that the Moreans were operating a company in their garage and they were very successful.

Shirley Dittmar Wilson (CHS 1945) said some of her kids went to high school with Bill Morean. Shirley said Mr. Morean and another man named "James" (James Golden) had formed a company (in 1966) named Jabil Circuits. After awhile Mr. Morean bought out Mr. Golden. Mr. Morean would hire neighborhood women to put computer circuits together in his garage.

Bill Morean graduated from CHS in 1973. He went to Western Michigan University and graduated in 1977. In 1978 Mr. Morean got sick and he called the family together. He turned the company over to his wife and the kids. The company was growing and they needed more room but Mr. Morean didn't want to move operations. Mr. Morean died in November of 1979. The company was moved to the Troy side of E. Elmwood, across from Clawson side. The company continued to grow and they moved to I-75 and Joselyn Road in Auburn Hills. Jabil Circuits eventually moved to St. Petersburg, Florida. Bill Morean hired a number of high school friends to work in the company and many of them became very successful.

Wikipedia, Internet encyclopedia, says the following:

> Jabil was founded in 1966 by William E. Morean and James Golden, in Detroit, Michigan. The company began by assembling circuit boards for Control Data. The Jabil name come from the combination of the founders' first names (James and Bill). The company's major break came in 1979 when Jabil won a large contract with General Motors. Since then Jabil's top customers include Cisco Systems (16% of sales), Philips Electronics (15%), Hewlett-Packard (11%), and Johnson Control.
>
> Jabil's facilities are located in U.S., Belgium, Brazil, China, U.K., Ukraine, France, India, Italy, Japan, Malaysia, Mexico, Hungary, Poland, Vietnam and Singapore. Jabil's non-North American operations accounted for 79% of net revenue in fiscal 2003. Chairman William Morean and his family own nearly 30% of Jabil.

With regard to William Morean, Wikipedia says the following:

> William Morean is an American businessman who is currently Chairman of Jabil Circuits, Inc., a leading producer of circuit boards. He is also a billionaire and a member of the 2006 Forbes 400.

In 2008, *Family Business*, which focuses on America's largest family businesses, listed Jabil Circuit, Inc., as #26. In 2003 they were ranked #51. It says:

> #26—Jabil Circuit, Inc.—Ownership: Morean Family—Founded: 1966—Revenues: $12.29 billion—Employees: 61,000—www.jabil.com
>
> Founded in suburban Detroit garage as a computer equipment maker. Founder's son William Morean, now 52, swept floors as boy and returned in 1977 at age 22 to run a one-client company upon his father's retirement. He was CEO from 1988 to 2000, when he became chairman. The company is now one of the Nation's top makers of printed circuit boards and other electrical components. Morean family owns about 15%.

Beth-Ann Morean

CHS 1971

Co-owner of

Jabil Circuits

Beth Ann Morean is the daughter of William E. and Audry Morean. Her brother is William D. (CHS 1973). They lived on S. Crooks and then S. Batchewana in Clawson.

Their father was co-founder of Jabil Circuits, Inc. in 1966. (See "William D. Morean" for additional information.) Beth was also one of the family members that helped in the transition when her father retired and the company was growing rapidly. Beth moved with the company to Florida where she worked for Jabil and got married.

In a May 22, 1998 article, The *St. Petersburg Times* noted: "Beth Morean was in charge of all the company operations; her brother, Bill was the salesman, making calls during the day and repairing the company's machinery at night. Together, they built the company from 100 employees to several thousand." (Note—2008 they had 61,000 employees)

In 1997 Beth Morean and her husband donated 1.2 million dollars to the St. Petersburg Arts Center.

Stephan Ross
CHS 1975
European Textile Entrepreneur

Steve Ross said his family lived on Nahma and then Stephen Street in Clawson from 1968 to 1978. Steve had four brothers and a sister: Don (CHS 1973), Jim (CHS 1974), Tim (CHS 1977), Judianne (Rochester High 1980), and Rick (Rochester High 1982) Ross. Steve attended both Clawson Junior High and Clawson High School. Steve swam on the swim team for 6 years for Coach Brian White. He said "White was a great inspiration and motivator."

Immediately after graduation Steve enlisted in the U.S. Army so he could qualify for the Vietnam GI Bill and could go to college. In 1977 the U.S. Army sent him to Germany. He met Max Falk while in the service. The two of them were discharged from the army in 1978.

In 1980 the two young men came up with a business venture, importing T-shirts from the United States and Egypt and selling them to GIs in Germany. Thus the Falk&Ross Group was formed. Steve never did go to college. A short while later Falk decided to return to the USA and was heading up Great American Sportswear. In 1981 Steve bought Falk's shares of their company. The business at that time was exclusive with the US military.

Since Steve took the company over, he has turned the small German company into an internationally leading company. In 1982 Falk&Ross Group Europe became one of the first eight European wholesalers of the brand Jerzees. In 1994 the brands Hanes and Result followed. Today Falk&Ross is a leading European textile wholesaler for promotional and corporate fashion.

The corporation grew to be the largest wholesale promotional clothing company in Europe with offices in 10 countries (currently expanding to 18 by the end of 2009).

In May 2009, Steve wrote "In these difficult times I will sell the company for more than the worldwide average for investment capital deals in 2008. And I will travel around the US and Europe doing business angel projects, helping young people to get their business life started. I am divorced with 4 kids, living in the US, England and Germany."

CIVIC LEADERS

Janet Crawford (Lusk)

CHS 1961

Development Coordinator — Detroit Institute for Children

Janet S. Crawford Lusk was born in 1943 in Ohio. Janet was the third of five children of Theodore and Beula Crawford. Silblings were Allen (Highland Park HS 1956), Judy (CHS 1958), Joyce (CHS 1963) and JoAnn (CHS 1971) Crawford. The Crawfords moved to Clawson in 1955 and lived on W. Selfridge. Janet was very involved in her high school, having served on the Student Council, National Honor Society and a member of the homecoming court. Janet graduated from Clawson High School in 1961, at which time she began a 37 year career with the Detroit Institute for Children. Janet married Ken Lusk (CHS 1961) and they did not have any children. Janet died in 2005 of cancer.

At the time of her death Ken wrote the following:

> Her thirty seven year career at the Institute began as an Orthopedic Secretary. Her exuberant work ethic and insurmountable spirit eventually earned her an appointment as Assistant Director in 1978. As the Detroit Institute's fortunes began declining, an increasing portion of the disabled children the Institute typically served were uninsured. Budgetary restraints threatened the Institutes motto 'No Disabled Child Turned Away.' The Board of Directors appointed Mrs. Lusk the new position of Assistant Director/ Development Coordinator.
>
> This gentle taskmaster assembled a small team which raised millions of dollars through foundations, endowments, and fundraising efforts. Janet was forever grateful for the help she received from many of Detroit's philanthropic families. Of particular note, she was extremely

grateful for the early encouragement and endorsement she received from Mrs. Edsel Ford. Mr. Ford once returned Janet's telephone call saying, "Now what do you want?", followed by an engaging chuckle. Peter Stroh once stated, "Janet makes people feel like kings and queens and work like pawns."

The Henry Ford II Memorial Golf Outing, now in its fifteenth year at the TPC Dearborn, and the Institute's participation in the Charity Preview at the North American International Auto Show are but two of the enduring events benefiting the Institute that were first nurtured by Mrs. Lusk and her small development team. After serving two years as the interim Director, declining health necessitated Janet's retirement in 1998.

Her sister JoAnn wrote: "She never would have branded herself a hero, but a hero she was, quietly 'paying it forward' on a daily basis, with no expectation for anything in return, other than the personal satisfaction it gave her. She was a gentle spirit, a true leader and organizer and the core of her family. She left a mark that will be forever inscribed on the hearts of all the children she helped and the family she loved and who will love her always and forever."

Edward Luttenberger
CHS 1961
Board President National Vietnam War Museum

In April, 2009 I asked Ed Luttenberger to share some of his memories of Clawson and his life afterwards. He replied as follows:

We moved to Clawson in 1953, where I joined the 4th grade class of Kenwood Elementary for the second semester. It was here I was to meet many of my classmates and friends of the next 8-1/2 years. After completing the 5th grade at Kenwood, my 5 block walk to school extended to a mile, as all of us moved to the old Junior High School for 6th through 8th grades. This was the first time for most of us to experience moving from room to room for different classes. I think among the most memorable experiences was having to go from a third floor classroom to one in the basement, at the other side of the building, by passing through the boiler room.

In 7th and 8th grades, we also got released for an hour for lunch, and could leave the school grounds. This meant being able to go across the street to the candy store, or trekking several blocks to the park across from the athletic fields to eat our sack lunches in a tree fort we'd discovered. Along with my close friends Jerry Pisani, Jim Rettig, and Kurt Schlotterbeck, we whiled away many pleasant days planning how we'd someday rule the world.

In September 1957, we made the leap across the street to the High School. Suddenly, all our status as the top of the food chain was turned upside down, and we were lowly freshmen. Upperclassmen tried, and sometimes succeeded in selling the unwary elevator passes for this two story building with no elevator, and played other pranks on the new kids. The majority of us survived unscathed and did unto incoming freshmen as was done unto us when we became upperclassmen.

During my four years at Clawson High I pursued a College Prep academic program, and maintained a grade point average high enough to qualify for the National Honor Society, along with 16 other of my fellow classmates. I had many teachers that I enjoyed, but I'd have to say my favorites were Mr. Jerry Bannister, my Chemistry teacher, and Miss Enid Freeman for both History and French. My favorite classes were the sciences, particularly Chemistry and Physics, but there were really no classes I disliked.

I had an active extracurricular life during high school which included freshman basketball, reserve baseball, track, golf, forensics, Chef's Club, Camera Club, Junior and Senior plays, and Junior Town Meeting. I also worked all four summers as a caddy at Birmingham Country Club where I acquired my addiction to golf.

During my years in Clawson, there was only moderate growth of the town, and almost everyone knew everyone else. Kids played ball and rode their bikes in the streets, you could walk anywhere and feel safe, and "Ike" was always the president. People today may disparage the *Leave It To Beaver* images of that period, but for me, growing up in Clawson in that era was very much like that—except for the part about mothers doing the housework in dresses and pearls.

After graduation in June 1961, that idyllic life passed, and a new era began for me.

Just over two weeks after graduating from Clawson High School, in June of 1961, I reported to the United States Military Academy at West Point, and was sworn in as a member of the class of 1965. I successfully completed my first year at the Academy, but ran afoul of the History Department during my second year. As a result, I was separated from the Academy in February of 1963 for deficiency in academics. In those days, if you failed a single class you were out of the Academy.

Following my return to Clawson, my parents purchased a business in a small town north of Pontiac, and I spent the next year and a half helping run the store, while trying to attend Oakland University. Since my eighty hour work weeks were not conducive to full time academics, I found myself on academic probation at Oakland. This, and my experience at the Academy, was not something I was used to, having been in the top 5% of my class all through High School.

In January of 1965, I put my academic career on hold, and enlisted in the U.S. Army. After basic training, I spent the next two and one half years at Fort Polk, Louisiana. During that time, I married my fiancée, a 1963 graduate of Southfield High, and we had a daughter. In October of 1967, I re-enlisted, and received orders for Vietnam.

From December 1967 to December 1968, I was assigned to Headquarters MACV based first in downtown Saigon, and later at Tan Son Nhat airbase north of the city. During that time, I met one of my old Academy classmates, who was assigned to the same unit, and he convinced me to apply for a direct commission as a second lieutenant, which I did prior to the completion of my tour.

Upon my return from Vietnam, I was assigned to Oakland Army Base, California. Within two months of my arrival, I received a call from Infantry Branch instructing me to take a pre-commissioning physical. After passing the physical, I was commissioned a second lieutenant, Infantry, in March 1969, and reported to Fort Benning, Georgia for my branch basic course. While at Fort Benning, I applied for flight school, and after spending four months at Fort Jackson, SC as a Training Officer in a basic training company, reported to the U.S. Army Primary Flight School at Fort Wolters, Texas.

I completed flight school and was awarded my wings as an Army Aviator in July of 1970, and then received a transition course to the CH-47 Chinook helicopter, prior to departing for my second tour in Vietnam. I was assigned to the 242nd Assault Support Helicopter Company, and spent 10 months flying various missions in Vietnam and Cambodia, until the unit was withdrawn in September 1971. During that time, I served as Assistant Motor Officer, Communications Officer, and Operations Officer, in addition to my flying duties.

Upon return from my second tour, I was assigned to the 15th Support Brigade at Fort Lewis, WA and served first as the assistant Personnel Officer and then Commandant of the Basic Leadership School for the brigade. In 1972 I was given the opportunity to serve as the Operations Officer for the start up of the 243rd Assault Support Helicopter Company, another Chinook unit that was formed at Fort Lewis, having been withdrawn from Vietnam the previous year.

In June of 1973, I was informed that I was to be separated from the service as a result of a "reduction in force" (RIF), and spent my last three months in service working as an intern for the airport manager at Boeing field in Seattle, where I wrote the Operations Manual for the airport.

Following my separation from the service, my family and I moved to the Bay Area (California) where I secured a position with Peterbilt Motors Company, in their Engineering Department. For the next thirty-three years, I worked for Peterbilt and its parent company, PACCAR, Inc., in various managerial capacities. In my career, I worked in engineering, manufacturing, training, marketing, sales, and information technology, retiring in June of 2007.

During my time in marketing (three separate assignments), I was the project lead for the development of several new truck models as well as an entire new line of conventional truck models (the ones with long hoods). I also helped develop a computerized system for truck salesmen to configure and order trucks for their customers. This came about because of a system I developed as Director of Training—one which allowed truck salesmen to do the engineering calculations necessary for determining a drive train for a customer's truck, using a TI-1500 portable computer.

Soon after starting at Peterbilt, I returned to my academic pursuits, and received an Associate degree in Business Management from Ohlone College, in Fremont, California, followed by a Bachelor of Science in Business Management at San Jose State University in 1980 (Member of Beta Gamma Sigma Business Honor Society) and a Master of Business Administration at San Jose State University in 1982.

In 1993, I moved with the company to Denton, TX; my wife (still with the original) and I have lived in the area ever since.

In 1995, the local chapter of the Vietnam Helicopter Pilots Association began a project to build a museum to honor the men and women who served in Vietnam. I joined that project, which quickly developed into The National Vietnam War Museum, and became one of the original members of the Board of Directors. I have served one term as board president, and am currently on my second term (non-consecutive) as vice-president. Beginning in October, 2010, I will again take over as president for a two-year term. In addition to serving on the Board, since 1998 I have served as the museum's Director of Communications.

In addition to The National Vietnam War Museum, I have served on the Board of Directors of the Greater Lewisville Community Theater, and am an active member of both the Vietnam Helicopter Pilots Association (VHPA) and the Fort Wolters Chapter of the VHPA, as well as the San Jose State University Alumni Association.

Paul Raine
CHS 1975
Attorney and Co-founder of the Greater Detroit Free-Net

I asked Paul Raine to write his recollections of his childhood in Clawson. If this doesn't bring back memories of growing up in Clawson, nothing will.

I mostly remember riding my bike all over Clawson. Little league baseball practices were held mostly at the Clawson Park, so I rode my bike there quite often. Games were also held at the Elementary Schools, so I rode my bike to the games as well. I would often walk or ride my bike to the A&W and the Dairy Queen. I remember both of those places being packed with kids after a summer baseball game. When I got older, I remember riding my bike to the Oakland Mall and on one sunny summer day, I rode all the way to Stony Creek Metro Park and back.

I went to Parkland Elementary on Grove street and remember the old Parkland School that was on Parkland street. I remember visiting the old school during the summer for painting little ceramic plaques. I think they used that school as a voting precinct for many years before they tore it down. Between the two Parkland Schools, towards Rochester Road, there was an area that the City would fill with water during the winter for an ice rink. I remember once walking home on my ice skates after dark, in tears because my feet were so cold. It seemed like we got a lot more snow back then, but perhaps that was because I was much shorter and the snow just seemed deeper.

Near Parkland School, at Bellevue and Grove, there was a well-worn path you could take from Bellevue west to Renshaw Street. Also, at the south end of Bellevue at Bauman, there was a path you could take into Royal Oak. Down that path, there was a large wooded area where we would look for snakes and salamanders under rocks and logs. I also remember that there was a woman who lived on Bauman. She often took her St. Bernard dogs for a walk while riding her bike.

I remember looking forward each year to the 4th of July celebration at Clawson Park. The event seemed huge back then. I remember when I was about 7 or 8 years old, I lost my $5 bill on the way to the Clawson Park on the 4th of July. I was devastated, but was pacified when my sister gave me some of her money so I could play some of the games at the park. I remember that I decorated and rode my bike in the 4th of July parade one year with baseball cards as noisemakers on the spokes that were held in place with clothes pins.

The Hinmans lived across the street from me on Walper. Their grandmother lived next door to them, so in the fall, we had two lawns full of leaves that we would pile up, then swing from a tree into the huge pile. I also have many fond memories of visiting the Hinman's cottage on Wiggins Lake in Gladwin on the weekends.

I bowled in a league at the Elk's Club in Troy on Saturday mornings for several years (ages 7-10, I think) Later, I joined a league at Thunderbird Lanes and distinctly remember the encouragement we got from the father of one of our bowlers—Mike Hinske (also a 1975 graduate). My first bowling experience was upstairs, between Class Pharmacy and the Milk Depot at 14 & Main. I remember that they had small bowling balls there, so perhaps it was duckpin bowling?

I remember when the Dunkin' Donuts was first built next to Renshaw's bar. I also remember that there was a transmission shop just south of 14 Mile Road on Rochester Road. The back of the shop was a great place to find ball bearings that we used as "steelies" when we played marbles. When I was 9, my dad bought me golf lessons at the Northwood Golf Course on the north side of 15 mile road, between Crooks road and the T-Bird bowling Alley. I remember the inside of the clubhouse had a long trough where they would wash the range balls.

One of my first jobs was as a caddie at the Red Run Gold Course in Royal Oak. We would sit around waiting to be picked as a caddie and would spend money on hostess pies and pop while we waited. I also worked at the McDonald's in Troy on Main street south of 15 mile. I remember that they would give three free items to employees on breaks. I would be so hungry after working there, I would get a Big Mac, Quarter Pounder and a large fry and then buy my own drink. I also worked at FairWay Tile & Carpet on 14 Mile just east of Main street. I remember we painted most of the inside of the store one year and I painted my initials all over the store. I'm sure if you were to inspect the place you'd find a few P.J.R.s there.

I remember the oil trucks that used to oil the streets before they were paved. One night, the Clawson police chased a car down Pare street and around the corner onto Walper. The car lost control and then smashed into the house next door, hitting the gas meter. My brother and I both slept through the event in our upstairs bedroom in our bungalow on Walper.

In high school, I remember cutting class to go to Burger Chef or Burger King with friends. I remember cruising the streets of Clawson in my beige 1964 GTO and later my yellow & black 1967 Camaro SS 396. I also had a 1973 Yamaha road bike and went on many motorcycle rides with Dan Banninger (now deceased), Doug LaPine, and others. I would often stop after school at the dry cleaner's where my girlfriend (now wife) Bev Serre worked. I would stop at Lim's Palace and get some Chinese carryout and then sit and eat and talk with Bev in the dry cleaners.

Paul went on to say that he graduated from the University of Detroit-Mercy School of Law and was admitted to the Michigan bar in 1997. He is an adjunct professor of Computer and Internet Law at the University of Detroit-Mercy School of Law. He also teaches at Walsh College in Troy, Michigan.

Paul is also a co-founder and past president of the Greater Detroit Free-Net. The Detroit Free-Net was among the nation's first free, open-access, community computer systems—sort of the Internet before the general public was allowed on the Internet. The network was pioneered by Tom Grundner (CHS 1963) when he was at Case Western Reserve University. At the time, neither person knew that the other was from Clawson.

Fr. Simon Stark

Guardian Angels
Missionary to Africa

Fr. Simon Stark was born in 1911 in Michigan to German/ Hungarian parents, Hugo and Francisca Stark. His siblings were Barbara (born 1918) and Hugo J. (born 1925) Stark. In 1920, the Starks were living in Detroit. By 1922 they were living in Clawson. The 1930 census shows they were living at 206 Pare Street.

The Starks attended Guardian Angels Roman Catholic Church, which was built about 1923 on Pare Street. Simon entered the seminary in the 8th grade. He attended the Holy Ghost Apostolic College in Bensalem, Pennsylvania. This is a preparatory school and seminary that taught boys from the 8th grade to their second year of college. The 1930 census shows Simon was attending school at Holy Ghost at the age of 19 years.

According to Simon's nephew, Chris Stark, Simon was the first Guardian Angels boy to be ordained a priest. He was a religious order priest for the Congregation of the Holy Ghost. Fr. Stark's ministry took him from tribal villages in British East Africa (Tanzania Territory and present day Kenya) during WWII to African-American communities in the south during the Civil Rights Movements of the 1960s. Fr. Stark's work dealt with the physical as well as the spiritual needs of the communities. Chris said it was his understanding that there was a mission named after Fr. Stark someplace in the old British East Africa.

One family story about Simon took place somewhere in Africa. Simon had made a still (presumably for medicinal purposes only) and had it heating up as he was conducting mass. The still exploded causing several... er... interesting questions to be asked.

While in Africa, Fr. Stark was riding a motor bike from village to village when he hit a pot hole in the road and crashed. He broke his hip. After nine years living in Africa, this injury forced him to come back to the States. He worked in New Orleans, South Carolina, Milwaukee, and ended up in Bay City, Michigan where he died in 1966. He had walked from one building to another and slipped on the ice and fell. He broke his leg and could not get up. He laid there for several hours before someone found him. He went into shock and died a week or so later.

On January 7, 2007, *The Good News*, a publication of the St. Anastasia Catholic Church, Troy Michigan, wrote as follows:

> As a parish community we are often reminded of the need for an increase in vocations. All of us are asked to include vocations in our daily prayers.
>
> For the past year we have handed a chalice from family to family to take home for a week and pray for vocations. The chalice was donated by our parishioner, Chris Stark, and had belonged to his late uncle, Fr. Simon Stark, a religious order priest for the Congregation of the Holy Ghost. Fr. Stark's ministry took him from tribal villages in Africa during World War II to African-American communities in the south during Civil Rights movement of the 1960s, bringing the Good News of Jesus Christ to the poor and impoverished...

Teri Takai
CHS 1966
Chief Information Officer State of California

Teri Takai had a sister, Sue Takai (CHS 1975). They attended Hunter School. According to Janice Satow (CHS 1965), at some point the Takai family moved to San Diego, California.

Janice said that she remembers being mistaken for Teri when she went north of 14 Mile Road. The Satows lived on the south side and the Takais lived on the north side. They both have Japanese heritage and wore glasses. Janice is 2nd generation American, she wasn't sure about Teri.

Teri went on to get a BA in mathematics and a MA in Management from the University of Michigan. She then spent 30 years of management and technology experience in the private sector. Teri also held senior positions at major corporations, such as Ford Motor and Electronic Data Systems (EDS), where she directed global information technology operations in several capacities.

In 2003 Governor Jennifer Granholm, of Michigan, appointed her to head the Department of Information and Technology for the State of Michigan. She was the first woman and the first Asian-American to head that department.

On December 6, 2007, Governor Arnold Schwarzenegger announced the appointment of Teri to Chief Information Officer for the State of California. In this capacity, she is a member of the State of California's Governor's cabinet.

She is also the President of the National Association of State Chief Information Officers.

LAW

Kyle Hayes
CHS 1993
National Police Officers Hall of Fame

Kyle Hayes is the son of Bill Hayes [1] (CHS 1963) and Barbara Fraser Hayes (CHS 1967). His siblings are Kevin (CHS 1990) and Eric (CHS 1995) Hayes. The Hayes' lived on Madison. Kyle played football, basketball and track through high school. Kyle attended Grand Valley State University and played football there as a punter. Kyle wanted to be a police officer. He left Grand Valley and went to Oakland Community College in the Law Enforcement Program. He received his Associates Degree and worked as a turn-key for the Wayne County Jail. After a couple years he moved on to Redford PD and then Pontiac PD. He joined Pontiac PD in November 1998 as a patrolman.

In February 2008, Kyle was laid off due to budgetary cuts. He was in the third and last layoff group. The department went from a maximum of 180 officers down to 62 when Kyle's group was laid off.

The saga began on June 24, 2008. Kyle was having a coffee with Officer Robert Elinski at a Pontiac coffee shop. Elinski was dispatched to a hit and run accident over the police radio. A pick-up truck had struck a little girl and her mother. Elinski headed to the accident scene. Kyle jumped in his personal car and headed down Joselyn Road. Kyle spotted the pick-up truck involved in the accident. The driver was running red lights as it traveled south down Joselyn towards the center of town. Kyle followed the truck

[1] Editor's note: Yes, the son of the author of this book.

and used his cell phone to call 911. The truck turned into a subdivision and was running stop signs. Kyle followed along and the truck turned onto a dead end street. The truck stopped at the end of the street and Kyle stopped behind it. The driver got out and Kyle ordered him to stop. The 18 year old male driver reached back into the vehicle and picked up a liquor bottle. Kyle thought it might have been a glass bottle but it later turned out to be a plastic bottle.

Kyle was close enough by then to reach out and grab the driver's shirt. He broke free when his shirt ripped and ran into an apartment complex. Kyle left his car running and door open as he gave chase on foot. Kyle was wearing Crocs and carrying his cell phone. He ended up running out of his shoes and dropped his cell phone near the truck. Kyle chased the man bare foot for about a quarter mile into the apartment complex and found the driver trying to hide behind a dumpster. Kyle held the driver down until Pontiac Officers got there to help him.

As it turned out the driver of the pick-up truck was driving a stolen vehicle. He pulled into a drive way to turn around and backed into a vehicle parked on the street. He sped away and struck a mother and young daughter who were trying to get into their car parked on the street. He knocked the mother down and ran over the 6 year old girl, killing her.

The driver, who was drunk, was arrested for drunken driving resulting in the death of the girl. He later pled guilty in court and is serving 27 years in prison.

The Oakland Press (Oakland County, Michigan) ran a story on July 30, 2008 that read: "A laid-off Pontiac police officer has received an award from the American Police Hall of Fame & Museum for his role in apprehending an Auburn Hills man accused of driving drunk and killing a 6-year-old girl." Later in the article it said: "Art Orofino, a Commerce Township resident and member of the American Federation of Police & Concerned Citizens, nominated Hayes for the Venerable Order of the Knights of Michael the Archangel award. ... 'Here he is, a laid-off police officer,' Orofino said. 'He didn't forget what he was trained to do. I thought that was amazing.'"

On Tuesday, Orofino presented Hayes with a patch, medal and plaque. Orofino said information about Hayes will be on public display in the 53,000-square-foot American Police Hall of Fame & Museum in Titusville, Florida.

Bristol Hunter
CHS 1943
Judge

Bris was born in 1925 in Clawson. His parents were James F. and Thelma M. Hunter. He was the oldest of four sons. His siblings were James (CHS 1945), Thomas (CHS 1948) and William (CHS 1949) Hunter. They grew up on Broadacre Street. Growing up Bris worked as a soda jerk at his father's pharmacy at the corner of 14 Mile & Main.

Bris enlisted in the U.S. Army in Sept. 1943. He went through basic training and eventually was shipped to Europe, arriving in January 1945. He was given credit for being at the Battle of the Bulge, even though he arrived at a transfer station the day before the battle ended. He did not see any action there. He did see action several times as the army moved towards Germany. He was under tank and missile fire numerous times but never under small arms fire. He was never injured.

Bris was discharged from the army and he entered the University of Michigan where he received his undergraduate degree in 1949. Bris tells the story that when he was at U of M he lived in a dormitory. There was a competition between dormitories sponsored by the school Intramural Program. Part of the activities was that anyone that didn't play intramural sports had to go to the gym and shoot 25 free throws. Anyone that knows Bris, knows he is very uncoordinated. Bris went to the gym and shot the 25 free throws. Bris said he couldn't remember how many free throws he made but he did know "The blind guy beat me!"

Bris then went to U of M Law School and graduated in 1952. He came back to Clawson as an attorney and set up a law practice. In 1959 he was elected as Justice of the Peace and held that position until 1963 when he was elected Clawson Municipal Court Judge, which was a brand new position that was just created. He was Municipal Court Judge from 1963 until 1978, when the cities of Clawson and Troy merged their courts and became the 52-4 District Court. Bris was District Court Judge from 1978 until 1992 when he retired from the bench.

Bris tells the story about one of his cases he had in Municipal Court. The defendant was on trial for being drunk. He was pleading his case before Bris and said "Really your honor, I was sober as a Judge," which brought the audience to laughter.

Another case that came to mind was a traffic case in District Court. The defendant was charged with driving through a gas station drive-way to avoid the traffic signal at Maple & Crooks. The defendant said the reason he did it was because he had to go to the bathroom very badly. Bris asked why he didn't stop in the gas station and use their bathroom. The defendant said he had used a gas station bathroom once before and he got the "crabs" from using the toilet. This also brought the audience and the court to laughter.

It reminds me of one of my cases, when I was a Clawson Police Officer, that was in front of Bris in the 52-4 District Court.

I was the detective in charge of a Criminal Sexual Conduct case that happened in Clawson. The defendant was charged with molesting his girl friend's 7 year old daughter. The defendant had told his friend Mike Mathy (CHS 1968) what he had done to the little girl and Mike was on the witness stand to testify to the conversation.

Mike was a Vietnam Vet and he had lots of physical problems because of his contact with Agent Orange while in Vietnam. He had tumors that would keep growing back. The defense attorney was being very aggressive. He was trying to discredit Mike by saying there was no evidence that Agent Orange causes cancer or Post Traumatic Stress Syndrome.

Mike had testified he had seven or eight doctors he was seeing for various issues. The defense attorney then began to ask Mike for their names and how to spell them. Mike listed 3-4 names and gave their spellings. He then had trouble spelling the rest of the doctor's names. The defense attorney seized the moment to attack Mike for his memory. When he asked again how to spell the doctor's names, Mike responded, "I don't know, I went to Clawson!" Nearly everyone in the court room broke into laughter and smiles.

Almost everyone in the court room had graduated from Clawson High School except for the pompous Birmingham lawyer who looked very perplexed. Bris graduated from Clawson; I graduated from Clawson; Joyce Whitaker Todd (CHS 1965) Oakland County Ass't. Prosecutor was from Clawson; Mike Mathy (CHS 1971) was from Clawson; the defendant, graduated from Clawson; the victim's mother (CHS 1971) graduated from Clawson and her daughter was a student at Kenwood Elementary in Clawson.

The case was bound over to circuit court and the defendant later pled guilty and was sentenced to prison.

David Hunter
CHS 1978
Author and Environmental Lawyer

David Hunter is the son of James and Ruth Hunter. He is the youngest of four children. His siblings are James (CHS 1970), Robert (CHS 1971) and Kathy (CHS 1973) Hunter. The Hunters grew up on John M Street.

David graduated from University of Michigan in 1983 and Harvard Law School in 1986. He is an Associate Professor of Law at American University in Washington D.C. He specializes in Environmental Law.

David has written at least ten books on financial and environmental issues plus many publications. He has given presentations all across the United States and many foreign countries in Environmental Law, Human Rights and Financial Law. A few of the countries he has given talks in are Belize, Peru, England and Cote d'Ivoire (the former Ivory Coast).

MILITARY

Edith Davis
CHS 1927
Pioneering Women's Army Corps Officer

In Melodie Nichols' publication, *Living History,* [Clawson Historical Museum Publication, Aug, 2008] is the following:

> Edith Mary Davis was born January 23, 1910 in Cleveland, Ohio. Her father was William Edward Davis and her mother was Edith Gade Davis. She had four siblings, Francis, Florence, Carol and Anna.
>
> The family moved to Clawson, Michigan in 1913, to the Reid's Hill area. William built the family home at 409 Webik Avenue. He worked for Ford Motor Company as a tool and die maker, and was a part-time mathematics instructor at Ford Trade School. Edith's mother was employed as a comparative shopper at Crowley-Milner in Detroit.
>
> Edith's mother died in 1926, and she helped her father raise her younger siblings. After graduation from Clawson High School in 1927, Edith worked at the Clawson Bank and a bank in Detroit before attending Alma College, graduating in 1934. She then completed a Master's course at the University of Michigan in Social work, receiving a Master of Social Work degree in 1950 from the University of Denver. Her Master's Thesis was on "Why Girl Scout Troops Lapsed: A Follow-up Study of Volunteer Leadership of Troops in the Denver Metropolitan Area, 1949."
>
> Of her military career, her own words can describe her many activities and distinctions, in a letter she wrote to her sister Carol's daughter, Roberta Bonning, in March 1979.

After graduation from Alma (1934-with highest honors-guess I like to brag) I entered social work in President Roosevelt's New Deal Programs—family casework in Royal Oak and Grand Rapids, Michigan with the FERA (Federal Emergency Relief Administration), then moved to Detroit and worked in a Community Center while I was studying part time in the social work Master's program at the University of Michigan. I also worked in Detroit's old age program was intake supervisor, then went with Roosevelt's work program (the WPA) in Wayne County as head of information and Adjustment Service and the Labor Relations Division. When World War II came along, I joined the first class of WAC (Women's Army Corps), became an officer and trained three companies of recruits at Ft. Des Moines. When they got ready to send women into the field, to posts, camps or stations, I took one of the first three companies out and we were the first white company to arrive.

This was at Ft. Sheridan, Illinois. From there I was assigned as an executive assistant and officer recruiter to the Sixth Service Command in Chicago. I had left Ft. Des Moines as a Captain (never was a first lieutenant—they jumped a few of us.) I was preparing for assignment to Company and General Staff School at Ft. Leavenworth when I was suddenly assigned to Ft. Devens, Massachusetts to pick up an overseas battalion.

Our ocean crossing was a long, tough ordeal—we were stranded in Newfoundland and Nova Scotia –took 6 weeks to reach Liverpool. That is a separate story. When we got to London I was put in charge of the American enlisted women in that city, just in time for heavy nightly bombings and other scary events. Within a few months I was asked to set up an integrated organization composed of American WACs, the three British Women's Services, nine ATS (Auxiliary Territorial Service) groups, Army, WAAF, Air Women, and WRNS (Navy), plus some Canadian CWAC and French underground. There was no blueprint for this kind of headquarters, which was being prepared for General Eisenhower, still in Africa. But we did get it organized with the help of American and British women officers—all told we had several hundred enlisted women in common living and eating quarters in Eisenhower's headquarters at Bushey Park, England, a London suburb. We also had women in our London billet.

In February, 1944 the Germans bombed our WAC section at Bushey Park—no casualties but a big mess. Later came the buzz bombs and we lost our London billet—a few WAC injuries but no deaths. Unfortunately, the GIs living in a house back of us were nearly all killed in that incident, which was around July 4, not long before D-Day.

The story of the women with (General) Eisenhower's headquarters in Europe is a long one, and I am planning to write it for the WAC Museum at Ft. McClellan, Alabama. We served in at least nine different locations, including Versailles, and ultimately Rheims, where the peace was signed, and Frankfort, Germany, after the fighting ceased and we separated from the British. Our women received several awards, including the Meritorious Service Unit Citations, battle starts, medals, etc. I received the Legion of Merit, and the Order of the British Empire. We also took many Jewish and Catholic Polish girls from concentration camps, and the officer I put in charge of that (now deceased) was awarded a special commendation by the Polish government.

Edith continued to distinguish herself after the war, completing her Master's work and teaching at the University of Denver, chairing a doctoral program, and receiving awards for her work. She continued to teach on a volunteer basis into her 70th year.

Edith died 29 July 2003 at Craighead, Arkansas. She never married.

Bud Trexler
CHS 1963
Army Commander/ West Point Professor

Herbert "Bud" Trexler, Jr. graduated from Clawson High in 1963. He has two children from his first marriage (Carol Brann—class of 1964). He and his wife Maggie and four dogs live in Cape Canaveral, Florida. Bud played football, basketball, baseball and track at Clawson. Bud retired from Lockheed Martin after 24 years in the aerospace business. He also had a parallel career retiring from the U.S Army as a Lieutenant Colonel while serving for 24 years.

Bud grew up at 670 Hendrickson. He started in the third grade at the old high school which was converted to the elementary school. For the 6th grade he had to transfer to Log Cabin Elementary located on Main Street near Fifteen Mile Road. The best way to school was through the undeveloped woods crossing into Troy and coming out on Main Street in Clawson. He joined the band, attempting to play the clarinet, and also became a Boy Scout.

For Junior High, he was transferred back to the old high school and started playing organized sports. Not being a good musician or scout, he gave up those activities and focused on sports—and chasing the cheerleaders.

After high school, Bud attended Eastern Michigan University where he stayed in school and graduated with his Master's Degree in math, with physics and chemistry minors. Bud worked for an engineering company in Ann Arbor while in undergraduate school and then taught math and science to inmates at Milan Federal Correctional Institute. His best math student was killed in a prison escape attempt in 1968.

Bud joined ROTC while in college and graduated as a Distinguished Military Graduate with a Regular Army Commission. He started his military career at Ft. Bliss (El Paso), Texas.

He served as a Commander of three different Army units including units at Ft. Bliss, Vietnam, and Korea. He was also fortunate to be assigned as an Assistant Professor of Mathematics at the United States Military Academy, West Point, New York.

When Bud was in Korea, his best friend from West Point, Captain Arthur Boniface, was assigned as Commander of the Demilitarized Zone, separating North and South Korea. Unfortunately, CPT Boniface was ax murdered by the North Koreans in August of 1976. Bud came into the national spot light and national news when he escorted the remains back to West Point.

While assigned to a project management position at Ft. Monmouth, New Jersey, Bud received a promotion to Major ahead of his Army contemporaries. He was selected to attend the Naval Command and Staff College—one of a select group of Army personnel to receive that prestigious assignments. Unfortunately, this successful career came at great sacrifice to his family since he would have to continue to be separated for a year every three years.

With his project management experience with aerospace and the Pentagon, Bud resigned from active duty after 12 years to join the Army Reserves. He started his career in aerospace in Boston but soon transferred to Florida to work for Lockheed Martin, the world's largest aerospace defense contractor.

Bud worked as an aerospace project manager for 24 years, rising to the Director level in executive production management. He stayed with the Army Reserves working in parallel with Lockheed. In the reserves, he worked in the Pentagon in a Research and Development assignment while also supporting West Point as a liaison officer for potential new cadets.

In his 24th year with Lockheed, while running a top secret cruise missile factory in Alabama, Bud suddenly became diagnosed with acute myeloid leukemia. Given three months to live, he and Maggie moved to Houston to receive a bone marrow transplant at the M.D. Anderson Cancer Center. He was diagnosed with a 25% chance to survive. During the next three years, he suffered through 16 surgeries, almost dying six times, and experienced many "speed bumps." Bud's leukemia is now in remission. The support of his wife, Maggie, kept Bud going. With God's gift, and

M.D. Anderson's superior technical medical talents, Bud has survived and is still alive "to fight another day."

During Bud's military career, he received numerous awards including the Silver Star for Gallantry in action, the Meritorious Service Medal, Bronze Star (twice), Air Medal, two Vietnamese Silver stars and many other awards.

At Lockheed Martin, Bud also received numerous awards including Manager of the Year.

Today, Bud and Maggie live in Cape Canaveral enjoying boating, camping, cruising, and traveling. They are thankful for their blessings and their family and friends.

SPORTS

Mark Campbell
Tight End — National Football League

Mark was born in 1975 and lived on Shenandoah in Clawson. His parents are John (Jack) & Betty Campbell. Mark was a football, basketball and baseball player at Foley.

He was on the Michigan High School All-State Football team and named as an All-American by the National Recruiting Advisor and listed him as the sixth-best tight end prospect in the nation. He was also named to the Parade magazine and BlueChip Illustrated All-American teams.

Mark went on to play four years for the University of Michigan as a tight end and was a three year varsity letter winner. He was one of five players to play in all 50 games during his career (Jon Jansen, CHS 1994, was one of the other players).

Mark is an American Football League tight end in the NFL for the New Orleans Saints (2006-2009). He has also played for the Cleveland Browns (1999-2002) and the Buffalo Bills (2003-2005).

Marty Clary
CHS 1980
Pitcher
Atlanta Braves

Martin Keith Clary was born in 1962 in Michigan. His Upper Deck baseball card says, Detroit, Michigan. He is the son of James & Mary Clary. He has two siblings, Monty Clary (CHS 1978) and Beth Clary (CHS 1982), a medical doctor. The Clarys lived on Pare Street in Clawson.

Marty was a three sport star for CHS. He played football, basketball and baseball. His father, Jim, was the varsity boys and girls basketball coach for Clawson. Brother Monte also played on the team. Both were very good players and their teams were very competitive. For a few years during that time period the local newspapers referred to the Trojans as "the Cardiac Kids." There were many close scoring come-from-behind victories. I witnessed many of these games. On one of these occasions I left the game, with my dad, Hugh Hayes, with about 90 seconds to play. Clawson was losing by 7 points. When I got to the parking lot and drove away I noticed that no one was leaving the school. The next day I found out that Clawson had come from behind to win the game.

Marty went on to college at Northwestern University of the Big-10 Conference. He played basketball and baseball for the Wildcats. I used to watch Marty on TV playing basketball for Northwestern and later pitching for the Atlanta Braves. He was drafted in 1983 by the Atlanta Braves in the 3rd round of the amateur draft.

He pitched for Atlanta from 1987 to 1990 when injuries to his pitching arm shortened his career.

In June of 2009 I contacted Marty and asked for an update on his life:

> Thanks for contacting me about Clawson. Monty is a guidance counselor and coach in Troy, like his Dad was in Clawson. I had the privilege to play with my brother and under our Dad on very competitive teams. I went to Israel with an organization called Baseball without Borders where we instructed players and coaches of all ages, but particularly youth in the fundamentals of baseball. I own two physical therapy offices, one in Piedmont and one in Easley, S.C. I am sole owner of the Velocity Sports Performance Building and business in Greenville, S.C.

Tim Gleason
Guardian Angels Defenseman — National Hockey League

Tim Gleason was born in 1983. According to Jeff Ross (CHS 1979) Tim's parents are Kevin and Katie Gleason. They live on Kenilworth Place in Clawson. Tim attended Guardian Angels School up to the 8th grade. He then attended Kimball High School in Royal Oak for a couple years before he finished his schooling in Windsor, Ontario. Tim is not to be confused with his uncle T.J. Gleason (CHS 1979).

Tim devoted his time to ice hockey. He played for the Windsor Spitfires in the World U/17 Tournament.

Tim was drafted twenty-third overall from the Windsor Spitfires in the first round of the 2001 NHL Entry Draft by the Ottawa Senators. Before playing any games with the Senators, Tim was traded to the Los Angeles Kings on March 11, 2003, for Bryan Smolinski. After spending three years in the Kings organization, Tim (along with Eric Belanger) was traded to the Hurricanes on September 29, 2006, for Oleg Tverdovsky and prospect Jack Johnson. Tim is still with the Hurricanes (2009).

Tim played for the United States in the 2008 World Hockey Championship.

Ray Hayes
CHS 1964
Defensive Tackle National Football League
1968 Super Bowl Champion New York Jets

Ray Hayes is the son of Hugh & Wanda Hayes. Ray's siblings are Bill [1] (CHS 1963), Dolores (CHS 1966), Don (CHS 1967) and Rhonda Hayes (CHS 1970). They lived at 134 Redruth. Ray married Linda Nascivera (CHS 1965). They have four children, Deanna, Kelly, Scott and Erin. Ray & Linda presently live in North Branch, Michigan.

Ray played football, basketball and track in high school. In his senior year he broke a bone in his hand and missed half the football games. He went to the University of Toledo on a full football scholarship and played for 4 years. His senior year he was placed on the College Honorable Mention All-American football team.

In 1968 Ray was a 12th Round Draft Choice of the New Jets. Ray was a 2nd team defensive lineman and played on the Specialty Teams. In the fall of 1968 the Jets were in Oakland to play the Oakland Raiders. George Tarnow (CHS 1963) met up with Ray. George worked for the Alemeda County Sheriff Department, which includes the city of Oakland. George took Ray and four or five teammates out for the evening. George decided to show them some excitement so he took them to a Hell's Angels bar.

---

1 Editor's Note: The author of this book, Bill Hayes, is Ray's brother. It might also be pointed out that Bill (not Ray) was Clawson's first First-Team All-State football player, overshadowing his little brother—at the time.

George said when they walked into the bar the patrons got out of their way and there wasn't one bit of trouble. The players were all about the same size, 6' 5" and 260—300 lbs. George remembers Ray ordering a Coke-Cola and no one said a word. That night George took them back to their hotel room. George was walking down the hall to leave and Weeb Eubank, the Jet's head coach was staggering down the hallway apparently inebriated. Eubank squinted at George and told him it was bed check time. Apparently Eubank thought George was on the team.

Later that day the Jets played the Oakland Raiders. It was the game sports writers later called the "The Heidi Bowl" and referred to Heidi as "The Most Hated Little Girl in America." Joe Namath made the Jets and the upstart American Football League essential weekend viewing. NBC found that out the hard way. The network's idea of must-see TV in 1968 was its made-for-television movie version of the classic children's story *Heidi*.

On Nov. 17, 1968, the Jets led the Oakland Raiders, 32-29, with 65 seconds left in the game. NBC programmers, due to contractual obligations with Timex, switched off the game at 7 p.m. to go to *Heidi* in cities east of Denver.

The Raiders came back to score two touchdowns in a span of three plays in that final minute, winning 43-32. Jets fans not able to see the finish thought their team had won, unaware of Oakland's comeback. Jennifer Edwards, the child star of *Heidi* and daughter of Blake Edwards, said she knew she was "the most hated little girl in America" for a night. *Heidi*'s lasting impact: NFL contracts with the networks now require games to be shown in a team's market area to the conclusion, regardless of the score.

Ray, with other members of the New York Jets and the Oakland Raiders later received "Heidi Dolls" and "Heidi lamps" from the manufacture Matell. The Jets later went on to win Super Bowl III against the Baltimore Colts. Ray received his full share of the pay-off ($20,000.00) and a Super Bowl ring.

Ray is presently in real estate in Lapeer County, Michigan. Last fall (2008) he was elected Deerfield Township, Lapeer County, Supervisor.

Andy Helmuth
CHS 1985
Drafted by Chicago Blackhawks

Andy Helmuth is the youngest child of Charles "Chad" and Mary Jane Helmuth. Andy's three older siblings are David (CHS 1972), Diane (CHS 1974) and Jeff (CHS 1979) Helmuth. They grew up on S. Manitou. Andy married Terri Turner (CHS 1986). Terri was the 1986 Miss Michigan Teen USA.

Andy was drafted in the 3rd round and 53rd overall pick by the Chicago Blackhawks in the 1985 Entry Draft of the NHL. He was a goalie. Andy played with the Ottawa 67s and the Guelph Platers from 1985 to 1988 but never made it up to the Blackhawks. One year his team won the "Memorial Cup" which is the top amateur hockey team award in Canada.

Jon Jansen
CHS 1994
Offensive Tackle National Football League

Jon, or as his mother likes to call him, Jonathan, played football, basketball, baseball and sometimes track at CHS. Jon is the son of Larry and Ellen Jansen. He has two brothers, Matthew (CHS 1992) and David (CHS 1996) Jansen. The Jansen's grew up on Darbee Court.

When Jon was a sophomore and Matt was a senior at CHS, they had a very good basketball team. Jon was 6'8" and Matt came in at 6'7." They both could do two handed dunks of the basketball, and there were five more people on the team that could dunk the basketball with one hand. This team went to the semi-finals of the Michigan High School Basketball Tournament which was being held at the University of Michigan. Matt had injured one of his legs during the season and kept aggravating it. By the time of this game he could barely walk. He tried to play but it was very painful. Lloyd Carr, football coach at University of Michigan, later told me this game is where Jon came to the attention of the U of M coaching staff. Jon played his heart out and showed a lot of tenacity even though Clawson was losing by a lot of points.

After high school Jon went to the University of Michigan on a football scholarship. Up to this point Jon had never missed a football practice or game while playing for Clawson Middle School or CHS. Once at U of M Jon was redshirted his freshman year, which was the normal practice at that time. Wikipedia, the Internet encyclopedia, says: "Jansen was a two-time First-Team All-Big Ten selection at Michigan. He set a school record with 50 straight starts, all at Right Tackle, earning the nickname "Rock." As a senior in 1998, he was named a First-Team All-American by the Burger King American Football Coaches Association. He paced Michigan's down lineman with 106 knockdowns on an offense that gained

4,955 yards. He helped Michigan to a 45-31 victory over Arkansas in the Citrus Bowl. He was Michigan's co-captain as a senior and junior and fortified an offense that posted 4,652 yards in route to the National Championship."

Wikipedia went on to say Jon was drafted by the Washington Redskins in the second-round. Jon started 82 straight games for Washington before he tore his Achilles tendon in the pre-season opener in 2004 against the Denver Broncos. He missed the 2004 season. In 2005 he came back to start all 16 games and two playoff games. Jon started all 16 games in the 2006 season. Jon suffered a season-ending broken and dislocated ankle in the season opener in 2007.

In May 2009 Jon was released from his contract with the Redskins. He was immediately signed to a one year contract with the Detroit Lions.

	**Tom Joyce** **CHS 1971** **Pitcher** **Chicago White Sox system**

Tom Joyce is the son of Charles A. "Boots" and Luella Joyce (CHS 1950). Tom has siblings Duane (CHS 1974), Margi (CHS 1982) and Jayne (CHS 1976) Joyce. The Joyces lived on Hendrickson.

After high school Tom went to the University of Michigan where he pitched for the baseball team. He was drafted 27th in the 1975 baseball draft by the Chicago White Sox. Tom pitched for the Appleton (WI) Foxes, farm team of the White Sox. He was released in 1976. There was a baseball trading card issued for Tom.

> My family lived on Roth and later moved to Hendrickson. I grew up and attended Clawson schools in grades K-12, graduating in 1971. I participated in sports all through my life beginning in little league up through varsity sports in high school. I played football, basketball and baseball in grades 7-12.
>
> I played in the sandlot baseball leagues in Detroit during the summers in high school. Some of the sponsors of those teams were Kowalski Sausage, Packer Pontiac and Adray Appliance.
>
> I attend the University of Michigan (1971-1976) and played baseball for four years. I was a member of the 1975 Big Ten championship team. I continued playing in the sandlot leagues in Detroit during the summers and also played in the Cape Cod college league in 1974.

In 1975 I was drafted by the Chicago White Sox. I played a short rookie league season in Sarasota Florida and an 'A' league season in Appleton Wisconsin in 1976. I was released in the spring of 1977.

I have been employed for the past 32 years with General Motors Powertrain working in the supply chain area of the business in plants located in Ypsilanti, Toledo Ohio, Romulus, and Warren.

I am married and have 3 adult children."

Thomas Morgan

CHS 1972

Olympic Sports Medicine

George Thomas Morgan is the son of George and Polly Morgan. Tom grew up on Broadacre Street.

In Tom's biography, he wrote he was originally from Knoxville, Tennessee. His family moved to Michigan in 1967. He graduated from Michigan State University in 1978 with a B.S. in Zoology and Physiology.

Tom attended Wayne State University for his medical training and graduated in 1982. He became board certified in 1986.

Tom did a one-month rotation at the Olympic Training Center in Colorado Springs, Colorado during his residency, and first became familiar with the Colorado Springs area in 1984.

He was the first Fellow in Sports Medicine at Michigan State University during 1985-1986 and one of the Team Physicians at M.S.U.

Following his Sports Medicine Fellowship he became an Associate Professor at the Medical College of Virginia. While there he and the core group of the Sports Medicine program were invited to the Soviet Union by the Soviet Olympic Committee to serve as the faculty for educational seminars for Soviet Olympic Physicians. This group donated and introduced the first arthroscope ever used in the Soviet Union in 1992.

Tom set up his private medical practice in Colorado Springs. He and his wife, Dr. Robin Morgan, lived on a ranch north of Colorado Springs, raised and trained English Pointer Field Trial dogs, Equestrian performance horses, and had a herd of Long Horn cattle. They own one National Champion English Pointer and 2006 & 2008 National Shooting Dog of the Year: Hannabell.

Tom says "Hannabell is our superstar." She is closing in on the all time greatest number of Open Championship wins, pro or amateur, in the highest level of competition in the Field Trial world, in the history of the sport. The sport began in 1886 in Western Tennessee.

Tom said his father raised English Pointers and beagles. That is what started his interest in dogs.

He said his family moved to Clawson the summer before he entered sixth grade. He attended Schalm Elementary. It was several years later that he met Jim Clary, Teacher/Basketball Coach at Clawson High School. Jim had grown up in Paris, Tennessee, not far from where the Field Trial sport started in 1886, in western Tennessee. Jim had won several championships with his dogs in the "Walking Field Trials." When Tom was a sophomore at MSU in 1974 his father died. Jim Clary became, and still remains, a second father to him.

Tom wrote,

> I want to tell you one story about Jim Clary. I was on the eighth grade basketball team. Bill Wentz, my coach, told Clary he needed to come watch me in a few of our games because Wentz thought I had some real potential. I had never met coach Clary. My dad and I had been to a few Varsity games at CHS but I had never met Mr. Clary. After the first game he saw me play in the 8th grade, he asked my dad, sitting next to him in the stands, if he (Jim) could take me to the Michigan High School semi-finals and finals that year to really get me juiced up about basketball. My dad said yes.
>
> "Mr. Clary waited for a few games before he came down out of the stands to introduce himself to me. He told me he had talked to my dad and asked if I could go with him the next Sat. night to watch Campy Russell, from Pontiac Central, play against Lindsey Harrison, from Detroit Kettering, in the Quarterfinals of the Michigan High School Boys Championships.
>
> "Of course I was honored and delighted. It was just "Coach Clary and me" and we may have been the only two white people in the gym that night. It was a simple but magnanimous gesture on Coach Clary's part. After watching the kind of game that those kids could play (6 out of 10

starters went on to play Division I basketball in college), I had a fire in me that drove me to become as successful as I could possibly become in any endeavor I chose to tackle. I, like everyone, have significant limitations in most things. But because of the work ethic instilled in me by my family, coaches, and teachers—and many great moments with Jim Clary and all of the other wonderful teachers and coaches at Clawson—I have never approached any challenge without the true feeling of confidence that I could climb any mountain as long as I was smart about it and worked like a mule!!" Tom became a third team All-State basketball team member his senior year of high school.

In April 2009, Shirley Dittmar Wilson (CHS 1945) told me that Tom had told her once he had read an article about someone criticizing teachers. He got mad and set up a grant fund for about eight years in the 1990s. He gave $5,000 each year to the fund to help teachers in the classroom. Teachers that were interested could apply for the money and explain how they would use the money. A three person committee would evaluate the applications and vote how much would be awarded to them. For a number of years Tom made the trip back to Clawson to award the money to the winning teachers.

Frank Niedowicz
Log Cabin High School
Class of 1944
Pitcher/Outfielder
Philadelphia Athletics system

Frank Niedowicz was born in 1926. He lived in Troy and attended Log Cabin High School, in Clawson. He was a member of the Class of 1944.

He was drafted by the Philadelphia Athletics and played at least three years with the A's farm teams. In 1948 he played with the Federalsburg, Maryland, A's; 1949 he played with the Moutrie, Georgia, A's and in 1950 he was with the Lincoln, Nebraska, A's. He was a pitcher/outfielder on these teams.

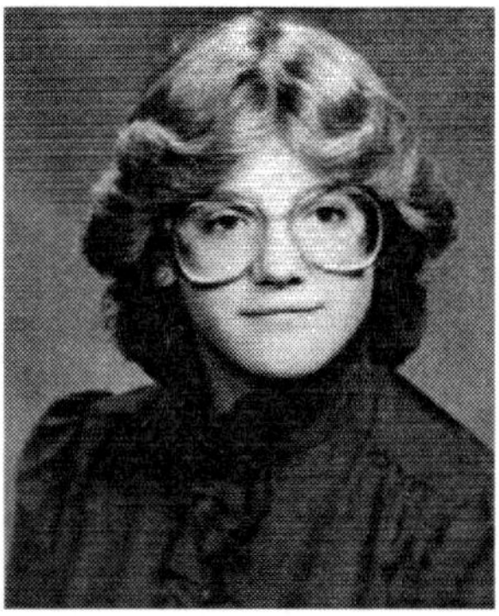

Mary Olsen
CHS 1983
Two time Big-10 Individual Gymnastics Champion

Mary Olsen is the daughter of Walt and Barb Olsen. They lived on Phillips Street. Mary has a brother Scott Olsen (CHS 1979)

Mary received a full athletic scholarship for gymnastics to Ohio State University. She was a member of the 1984, 1985, 1986 and 1987 teams which won the Big-10 gymnastics championship all four years. Mary was All-Big Ten 1st team all four years, winning the Big-10 All-Around Individual title in 1984. In 1985 she won the Big-10 Individual Uneven Bars, Balance Beam and Individual titles. In 1986 she won the Big-10 Individual Uneven Bars title.

Mary was working towards the 1988 Seoul Olympics; however, it didn't work out. She married Greg Wiedbusch in 1991.

Gary Sabaugh
CHS 1975
Pro Wrestling Federation Heavyweight Champion

Gary Sabaugh is a professional wrestler known as "The Italian Stallion." He grew up on N. Main Street in Clawson. He wrestled in high school for Coach Roman "Ray" Podulka, aka "Pud".

Gary lives in North Carolina and wrestles in the PWF (Pro Wrestling Federation). Most of his notable bouts were in the 1990s against "George South," "The Universal Soldier," "The Big Unit," and "Bloodsucker." In 1990 he defeated the "Russian Assassin" for his first PWF Heavyweight title. He had 17 other individual and tag team wrestling championship wins up to 1999 when he and "Brutus McNasty" defeated "The Soul Searchers."

But just in case you think professional wrestlers can not actually wrestle, consider the following written in the "Scholastic Wrestling News," March 1, 1977:

> Clawson Senior High, Clawson, Mich.
> New Record: Most Falls by a team, single season
>
> The Clawson Senior High School team of Clawson, Michigan, recorded 156 falls during the 1974-1975 season. This total betters the existing mark of 117 by Stevens High of Rapid City, South Dakota. The Clawson team finished 11-0 in duals and third in the Michigan State Tournament. 51 of the pins came in dual and 105 in tournaments (9). Top pinners were 98 pounder John Ball (41-3) with 33, heavyweight Gary Sabaugh (37-8) with 25, and 126 pounder Bob Sade [1] (42-1) with 25.

[1] Bob Sade is the younger brother of Joe Sade (Bishop Foley HS 1971),who is also in this book as an Olympic wrestler.

Joseph Sade
1976 Olympic Wrestler

Joe Sade, Jr. is the son of Joseph and Helen Sade. He was the oldest of four brothers and a sister, Bill (member of CHS 1972), Bob (CHS 1975), Chris (CHS 1977) and Carol (CHS 1980) Sade. They lived on the third block of Redruth.

Joe was the 1971 Michigan champion at 112 lbs for Bishop Foley High School, Madison Heights. Bill Wentz, retired Clawson Middle School teacher, said Joe Sade was a student of his in the 1967 school year.

In 1973 Joe was in the FILA World Championship Greco-Roman representing the U.S.A. He wrestled at 125 lbs.

He went to college and wrestled for the Oregon Ducks. In 1975 & 1976 he was the PAC 10 Individual Champion at 125 lbs.

In 1976 He was on the U.S.A. Olympic Greco-Roman Wrestling Team and wrestled at the Montreal Olympics at 57 kg (125.5 lbs). Joe told me he lost his first match to a Czechoslovakian. He won his next two matches, the first against a Mongolian and the second against a Portuguese opponent. His final match was against a Japanese wrestler. They were tied towards the end of the match when he was suddenly pinned by the Japanese wrestler. If Joe could have won that match he would have been guaranteed a bronze medal.

In 1976 Joe was placed in the National Wrestling Hall of Fame in Stillwater, Oklahoma.

I remember Joe riding a skateboard around town, being pulled by his two Walker Hounds, Scooter and Skeeter. The dogs were wearing harnesses and had a double lead. The dogs really seem to enjoy what they were doing. Their tongues were hanging out and they had the biggest smiles on their faces. They would really be straining to get the skateboard to move but once it did, away they would go. This would have been near the time of the 1976 Olympics.

Joe Sade wrote the following June 2009:

> After Clawson High School's last football game of the 1969 JV season, I overheard Ray Podulka tell Brian Crookshank (lineman) he should come out for wrestling. It caught my interest and I tried out. The very first practice, I separated my shoulder. Captains Don Songer and John Chuddy convinced me not to quit. I missed two months of the season and finished at 7-7 at 112 lbs.
>
> Over the summer, at the invitation of my friend, Jim Brennan, I wrestled in a few open tournaments. Bishop Foley coach Art Roberts was at one of these and approached me, "You come to Bishop Foley," he said, "and I'll make you a state champion." I went and he made good on his statement. I finished my senior year at 35-0 winning the 112 lb state title.
>
> I went on to attend my freshman year of college at Eastern Michigan and finished the season at 22-2-1 with All-American honors.
>
> I then transferred to the University of Oregon where I finished my college career winning two Pac Eight championships.
>
> In 1973, I won the AAU Greco Roman nationals. I then made the US team and wrestled in the World Championships in Tehran Iran. While in Iran, I ran into an American couple at the street bazaar. Upon talking to them, I discovered they lived in Clawson only a couple blocks from my parents' home. Small world!
>
> In 1976, I made the US Olympic team at 125.5 lbs and finished in the top 10, winning two matches and losing two.
>
> In light of all this, the most notable moment in my life was when I became a born-again Christian in 1973. Jesus Christ has influenced every part of my life since. All the athletic ability, or any other ability I have has come from Him. I have since worked as a logger, a carpenter remodeling old houses, and currently own a carpet and upholstery cleaning business here in the Upper Peninsula of Michigan.

Stanley Somers
CHS 1947
Pitcher — Philadelphia Athletics

Stanley Somers was the son of Samuel and Claire Somers. His siblings were Doris (CHS 1942), Al (CHS 1947) and Larry (1951) Somers. Al Somers told me that in 1947 his mother was the president of the Clawson School Board and she handed him his diploma when he graduated. Laughingly Al said that was probably the only reason he got the diploma.

Stanley Somers signed with the Philadelphia Athletics after high school. He was a left handed pitcher. Al Somers said after a couple years Stanley left to enter the military and the Korean War. After his military duty was over Stanley rejoined the Philadelphia organization. He was assigned to the Fayetteville A's (North Carolina) for the 1952 season. 1953 he played with the Fayetteville team and the Hopkinsville A's (Kentucky) team. 1954 he was assigned to the Reidsville A's (North Carolina)

Bill Stewart
CHS 1946
Outfielder — Kansas City Athletics

Bill Stewart told me that he lived on a farm on W. Big Beaver, Troy, where the present day Drury Inn is located. The family moved to Clawson when Bill was in the 10th grade. After graduating from CHS, Bill went on football scholarship to Michigan State University.

Bill left school early and enlisted in the service along with four other friends. At that time they could enlist and serve 18 months. If they were drafted they would have to serve 24 months. In 1948 Bill was signed by the Philadelphia Athletics as an outfielder.

Bill played minor league baseball for 13 years. He played a year in Panama, a year in Mexico and a year in Cuba. By 1955 the Philadelphia A's had moved to Kansas City and became the Kansas City A's. He was brought up to the A's in April 1955. He played a month and a half in Kansas City and then he was sent back to the minors with the promise from the manager that he would be brought back up towards the end of the season. He broke his wrist a short time later and was never called back up, but he continued to play minor league baseball for several more years.

Brian Woltman
CHS 1975
Third Baseman
Houston Astros system

Brian Woltman was the son of Clibert and Mary Woltman. Brian is the fourth of five sons. His siblings are David (CHS 1971), Charley (CHS 73), Keith (CHS 1974) and Greg (CHS 1977) Woltman. They grew up on W. Elmwood across from the Clawson City Park.

Brian was drafted in the 17th round of the 1975 amateur draft by the Houston Astros as a 3rd baseman. Brian played one year in the minor leagues and according to his brother, Dave, had a career-ending injury.

Dave Woltman (CHS 1971) said Brian had played in a high school All-Star baseball game at Tiger Stadium in Detroit in 1975. Brian hit a home run over the fence during the game.

WRITING AND PUBLISHING

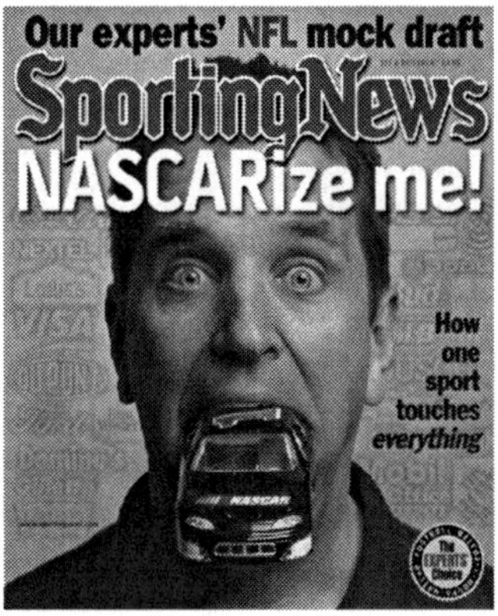

Matt Crossman
CHS 1990
Associate Editor — Sporting News Magazine

Matt Crossman was featured in a Central Michigan University weekly series of their most successful alumni (2005). He was on the cover of *Sporting News*, the oldest weekly sports magazine in America. Crossman attended CMU from 1990-1994, double majoring in Journalism and Political Science.

In May 2009 Crossman wrote:

Matt Crossman, 10/9/1971, Class of 1990. I lived in the same house on Oakley Street from birth until I went away to college. I have three brothers who all graduated from Clawson, too—Mike, 1987, Jim, 1991, and Bob, 1994. Parents: Dick and Kay Crossman.

I became a journalist because I am curious, I like to learn new things and I enjoy writing. Teachers at Schalm Elementary School, Clawson Middle School and Clawson High School recognized all of that and encouraged me along the way. Of course, in those days "curious" sometimes meant "talking in class" and "learn new things" meant "about what the kid behind me did the night before" and "enjoy writing" often meant "I will not talk in class" 1,000 times.

But everything worked out in the end. I was pretty sure back then that I knew what I wanted to be when I grew up, and everything I heard from my teachers reinforced my goals. In different ways, Mrs. Math (5th grade), Miss Schram (German), Mr. Dickinson (middle school and high school English) and Mrs. Evans (English) made me believe I could become a journalist. Corny as it sounds, that's all I've ever wanted to do.

I initially pursued a career writing about politics—my love of which I trace directly to Mr. Bruce's government classes. After a few years of that, life circumstances led me to write about sports, my love of which I trace directly to games played at Baker, Parkland, Schalm, City Park West, the street in front of my house, etc.

It didn't matter where I was—I could never hit a curve (or a fastball, for that matter). But I can write about others who can—I've written more than 30 cover stories in national magazines, the vast majority of them in *Sporting News*. My claim to fame is that I'm the only writer in the 123-year history of *Sporting News* to appear on the cover. To do so, I had to cram a plastic car in my mouth. To which some of my teachers would say, "I wish I had thought of that."

The thing I love and miss most about Clawson is the size. The high school is small enough that I knew everybody, teachers included, yet big enough to offer a wide variety of classes. The city is small enough that my dad put the siding or windows or gutters on roughly half the houses—and big enough that doing so kept him busy for years. Clawson is small enough that I could ride my bike everywhere, yet it's big enough to have its own massively cool fireworks on the 4th of July.

As a side note I learned that Jeff Gordon (CHS 1975) also lives and works in St. Louis. Jeff is a writer for the *St. Louis Post-Dispatch* and a radio host on a local station. Matt said he has been in the same sports box with Jeff and has listened to him for the last 8 years on the radio, but he does not know him personally. He was not aware that he and Jeff graduated from the same high school.

Molly Glad
Home Schooled Children's Writer

Molly Glad was born in 1983. She is the daughter of Dave and Pegge Glad and they live on Roth Blvd. in Clawson. Molly has a sibling, Emily. Molly wrote, "My sister's name is Emily and she is the same age as me—we're twins! However, we are eight minutes apart, four minutes before midnight and four minutes after. So we have different birthdays!" Molly and her sister were home schooled.

Molly wrote a children's book *The Night the King Couldn't Sleep*. The book was published by Tate Publishing and is presently on sale on Amazon.com and Borders. On March 15, 2009 Molly had a book signing and read the book to children at a newly opened coffee shop, Cuppy's, in Clawson. Molly said she did what she likes best, read to children. She told some stories and ended with reading her book.

Molly says she always enjoyed writing. She put together the story with drawings while at Wayne State University, studying for her bachelor of fine arts degree. She graduated Magna Cum Laude.

A class on Esther in the Bible inspired her to imagine what might have happened on that night long ago when the king couldn't sleep. Her story includes a scribe reading a bedtime story to the king and the chef bringing him cherry pie.

I remember Mrs. Glad and the two girls walking to Clawson City Hall several times a week to use the pay phone and talk with many of the employees that were working. This would have been in the late 1980s as the girls were young. The girls had very blonde hair and they were easy to spot.

Molly was asked what she thought about growing up in Clawson. She responded by writing:

> I loved growing up in Clawson, a place where you can walk anywhere you need to go. Living in a one car family for most of my childhood years, this was extremely convenient.
>
> I recall fondly:
>
> The July 4th celebrations, how family and friends would gather with us at Clawson park to see the phenomenal display of fireworks. Our town may be small, but it's mighty.
>
> Going to the Clawson Historical building with my mom and sister and playing the player piano.
>
> Walking to City Hall to use the pay phone, so that Mom could make long-distance calls to her sister.
>
> The joys of summer, the car festival, going to the Dairy Queen, or riding our bikes up and down our street and playing with the neighbor kids.
>
> Sitting by our front window and watching for our friendly and punctual mailman.
>
> The big snow shovel trucks making their way down our street in the winter. Our Clawson streets were always plowed well before my friend's in nearby cities.
>
> And today, whether it's helping with an election as precinct inspector, or with other civic activities, I love being involved in my city and having that sense of community you find in small town America—in the two square miles of Clawson nestled in the metropolis of Detroit.

Molly goes on to talk about her book and how busy she is with promotions and book signings. She wrote, "I am proud to say that my hometown library of Clawson was among one of my first story venues. As I continue with my writing and passion for childhood literacy through story time events and reading programs, I am proud to call Clawson my hometown and where, at the end of the day, I come home."

Jeff Gordon
CHS 1975
Sports Columnist/TV & Radio talk show host

Bill Wentz, retired Clawson Middle School teacher, says that Jeff is the step-brother of Pam Coutilish (CHS 1974). Pam is also listed in this book. Jeff & Pam also have another sibling, Cindy Coutilish.

Jeff is an online sports columnist for the Missouri *St. Louis Post-Dispatch* newspaper. He serves as president of the St. Louis Newspaper Guild and is a talk show host at KFNS-AM with a program called *The Gordo Zone*. He also is a national writer for FoxSports.com and MSN.com.

Previously he worked at the *Baltimore News American* and the St. Joseph, MO *News-Press and Gazette.*

In May, 2009 Jeff sent me the following about his recollections of Clawson.

> My father, David, is a retired UAW executive living in Grosse Point Woods. My stepmother Patty died in 1975. Step-sister Pam Coutilish (CHS 1974) is an actress, director, writer and drama teacher in New York City. She earned her degree from Eastern Michigan University. Step-sister Cindy Coutilish (member of CHS 1972), is a drug and alcohol counselor in suburban Detroit.
>
> I credit Mrs. Dutton (Creative Writing, Journalism) and Mr. Bruce (Government, International Relations) at Clawson High School for preparing me for college. They were phenomenal teachers. Both took a huge interest in me. Mrs. Dutton sent me to numerous workshops and Mr. Bruce opened my eyes to a lot of great current affairs writing. Mr. Clary, my counselor, got me involved with the bas-

ketball team as a statistician and prodded me to pick up my grades—which I finally did.

My good friend Chuck Hill (CHS 1975) got me involved in coaching a youth baseball team in Clawson's league. Among the players we faced was Marty Clary (CHS 1980), who later pitched in the major leagues for Atlanta. Make sure you get Marty in the book.

After graduating from CHS in '75, I went to the University of Missouri-Columbia to study journalism. I graduated in '79. I got a call to interview at the *Royal Oak Tribune*, but I already took a sports writing job in St. Joseph, Missouri, at the *News-Press and Gazette*. And thus began the journey . . .

I later moved on to *Kansas City Magazine*, then the *Baltimore News American* before coming to the *St. Louis Post-Dispatch* in 1986. I am currently the on-line sports columnist for our web product, STLToday.com.

I have written several sports books and been published in numerous periodicals, including *Sporting News* and *The Hockey News*. I have written for many national websites, including MSN.com, FoxSports.com and CBSSports. com.

My fondest Clawson memories came at the annual Fourth of July picnic, which was always a big deal. The city always did it up right for that holiday.

My least favorite memory was an armed robbery at the Burger King in 1974. I got stuck in a meat locker, along with Heidi Palmer, the mayor's daughter, and others. That was jarring.

As a side note I learned that Matt Crossman (CHS 1990) also lives and works in St. Louis. He is a writer for *Sporting News*. Matt said he has been in the same sports box with Jeff and has listened to him for the last eight years on the radio, but he does not know him personally. He was not aware that he and Jeff graduated from the same high school.

Tom Grundner
CHS 1963
Author / Publisher

Tom lived at 411 Gardner Street, on the northeast corner of Gardner and Bellevue. Son of Emil and Ann Grundner, he had two brothers, Larry and Ken, both of whom graduated from Grosse Point High before the family moved to Clawson. Tom lettered in football, basketball, baseball and track in school—which were the only sports we had at the time. In football, he was the offense left end. I played next to him as the left tackle. Tom was always trying to analyze everything and everyone, so it seems he went into the right profession.

Here is a literary "bio sheet" he sent along with the note: "This is more than any rational person could possibly want to know about me. Use whatever you want."

> Writing has become a "second career" for Tom Grundner— or maybe a third or fourth career, depending on how you count them.
>
> A native of Clawson, Michigan (a small town north of Detroit), Dr. Grundner received his undergraduate degree in Psychology from Eastern Michigan University; a Master's degree in Human Learning from the Institute for Behavioral Research in Silver Spring, Maryland; a second Master's in Education from the University of Southern California; and a doctorate in Educational Philosophy and Psychology, also from USC.
>
> For most of his academic career he was on the faculty of Case Western Reserve University, School of Medicine, in Cleveland, Ohio. While there, he participated in the devel-

opment of some of the earliest Internet applications. Indeed, several of the Internet services we now take for granted have their origins in his pre-World Wide Web work.

After a stint as the head of a non-profit organization, in 1998 he formed a for-profit company, Marietta Golf Products. The success of Marietta Golf allowed him to devote himself increasingly to his "first love," writing.

His academic books have ranged from the ethics of human experimentation (*Informed Consent*, 1986), to the problem of Internet pornography (*The Skinner Box Effect*, 2000). More recently, he was the co-author, with noted golf club designer Tom Wishon, of the award winning best-seller: *The Search for the Perfect Golf Club* (2005), followed by *The Search for the Perfect Driver* (2006), and *The Right Sticks: Equipment Myths That Could Wreck Your Golf Game*.

In 2007 he published *The Ramage Companion*, a companion book to the 18-volume series of historical novels by the British author, Dudley Pope, along with the first two books of a nautical fiction series based on the life of Admiral Sir Sidney Smith (*The Midshipman Prince* and *HMS Diamond*). The third book in that series (*The Temple*) was released in July, 2009.

Also in 2007, he became Senior Editor for Fireship Press (www.FireshipPress.com) a small publishing house that specializes primarily in nautical and historical, fiction and non-fiction, books. A second imprint (Cortero Publishing) opened in 2009.

His interest in the 18th Century British Navy was spawned during his years in the U.S. Navy. Eventually rising to the rank of Lt. Commander, he served a tour of duty in-country Vietnam doing coastal surveillance and coordinating swift boat patrols in the II Corp region. While there, he won the Navy Commendation Medal with Combat "V," the Vietnamese Gallantry Cross with Palm, the Vietnamese Civil Action Honor Medal, a Presidential Unit Citation, a Combat Action Device, and "a bunch of other gee-dunk medals" (as he calls them).

Sandwiched in-between all the above...

He was one of the nation's first newspaper computer columnists—writing a weekly column for the *Cleveland*

Plain Dealer beginning in 1983, and for several years he was a talk show host on radio station WERE in Cleveland.

Among his many honors and awards: In 1995, he was named by *Newsweek* magazine as one of the "50 Most Influential People in Cyberspace" (see also the *Newsweek* feature article on his work in their 6/26/95 edition).

He has received the Alumni Achievement Award from Eastern Michigan University, the Award of Achievement in Education from *Northern Ohio Live* magazine, was selected as an Outstanding Young Man of America by the U.S. Jaycees, and in 1984 was selected as one of the "Eighty-four Most Interesting People in Cleveland" by *Cleveland Magazine.*

In college, he was a record-breaking wide receiver at Eastern Michigan University and played several seasons in the old Midwestern Professional Football League for the Ann Arbor Vikings and later the Pontiac Firebirds.

I might add that his three novels are heavily laced with character names based on his Clawson High School classmates. As he says: "Hey, I had to name the characters *something,* so why not..." All three novels, as well as his golf books, are in the Clawson Library; and they are available via amazon.com, and via all the major bookstores.

CLAWSON TO CLAWSON

Robert Acton
Log Cabin High School 1945
CHS Teacher/Coach/ Friend

Bob Acton grew up in Troy, Michigan. He lived on Livernois, one-half mile north of Maple Road. Log Cabin High School was on Main St. (Livernois), two blocks south of Maple, in Clawson City limits.

Bob played all the sports he could in school. In April 2009, Shirley Dittmar Wilson (CHS 1945) said she always marveled at the students at Log Cabin. There were only 14 students in the senior class of 1945, half of them boys, or as Bob says "there were 7 boys, 6 girls and we weren't sure of the last one." The school fielded a football and basketball team and won most of their games.

When Bob graduated, he spent one year in the Merchant Marines and then two years in the US Army. He was a paratrooper stationed in Japan with the 11th Airborne Division. He then went to Alma College and graduated.

Bob began teaching in Clawson in 1952. He taught high school algebra and geometry. He coached football, track, basketball and baseball. His 1962 football team was one of the best in the state that year. With the help of assistant coaches Bob Hamilton and Ken Gibbard (CHS 1954), the team ended up 7-1. They scored 244 points to their opponents 26 points.

The 1963 Cavalcade (Clawson High's Yearbook) says the following:

> Not since 1957 has the Oakland B now (A) experienced the ferocity of a Clawson team.
>
> Clawson High is very proud of their grid contenders, who won 7 and lost 1. Our team crossed their opponents' goal line 4 times (should be 9 times) to every once they

> crossed ours, shutting out 5 teams and boasting one of the best defenses in the state.
>
> Fate works in a strange way. In 1962 Clawson and Troy had the 2 best Oakland "A" teams. On a bitterly cold October night our Trojans met their northern rivals on Troy's field, losing their hopes for a Conference Championship by 6 points.
>
> Thank you Mr. Acton and Mr. Gibbard, for that powerful line; and thank you Mr. Hamilton for those well trained backs. Last but not least, thank you Class of '63 for those outstanding athletes.

Going into this game Clawson was ranked 3rd in the state in Class B. Troy was ranked in the top 10 in Class A. Troy won 13 -7 in a hard fought game before an estimated 5,000 fans. Clawson ended up ranked 8th in Class B and Troy went undefeated and ranked near the top of Class A.

I remember a couple stories about Bob coaching football. Bob always seemed to have a cardboard tube about a foot long. He would use white athletic tape to wrap the tube, with knobs on the ends. We jokingly would refer to his weapon as "The Ugly Stick." Bob would use it to hit the top of our football helmets, while our heads were in it, to get our attention, or hit his free hand to try and make a point about what he wanted done. It was all harmless, but it did make us pay attention.

Another incident happened at the half-time of a football game. We weren't playing very well but happened to go ahead towards the end of the first half. Bob was laying into us about how we were playing. He was really using "The Ugly Stick" a lot at that point. However, one thing about Bob, he never used cuss or swear words around us. Bob continued to rant and rave. Unbeknownst to us was that Bob Birch (CHS 1963) had put a tape recorder in his locker and turned it on. While Bob was giving his half-time chewing out, Birch was sweating out what he had done. Coach Bob Hamilton had moved over close to Birch and Birch thought Hamilton could hear the recorder working. We went out for the second half and won the game handedly. The next day Birch brought the recorder out and everyone listened to the speech. Forty years later the recording was put on copies of game films from 1962 and dispersed to Bob and members of that team, where it has become a treasured remembrance.

Seven members of Clawson's team went on to play college football and one of them played with the New York Jets when they won Super Bowl III. The 1963 members were Bill Hayes, Alma College; Tom Grundner, Eastern Michigan University; Tom McArthur, Kalamazoo College. The 1964 members were Jack Ahlfeld, Kalamazoo College; Brodie Burton, University of Wyoming; Bill Kerr, University of Wyoming; and Ray Hayes, University of Toledo & the New York Jets.

Bob married Ferol Patrix (CHS 1957) and they had four children, Scott, Jeffrey, Lisa and Bill.

Bob left teaching in 1966 and became Assistant Principal of CHS for two years. He then became Principal of Clawson Jr. High for two years. From there, he left Clawson and became Principal of Clintondale HS for two years. In 1970, he was elected to the Clawson School Board. He spent several years as Assistant Superintendent of Oxford Schools and then moved on to join his brothers in the family business, Acton Trucking in Oxford.

Whitney Hames
CHS Teacher

Whitney Hames was born in 1897 in (the future Clawson), Troy Township, Oakland County. Whitney was a third generation Troy Township resident. His paternal grandparents Hiram (b. 1821 in New York) and Emily (b. 1828 in New York) Hames migrated to Michigan before 1855. They show up in the 1880 Troy Township, Oakland County, census along with three children, Elizabeth (b. 1855 in Michigan), Charles (b. 1866 in Michigan) and George (b. 1868 in Michigan) Hames. Fourth child Rhoda (b. 1858 in Michigan) had already married Allen Hendrickson by 1880 and they lived in Troy Township.

George and Ida Hames were Whitney's parents. The 1900 & 1910 Lamotte Township, Sanilac County, Michigan census shows the George Hames family was living in that township.

In handwritten notes from Whitney Hames, he said he graduated from the 8th grade at the Pidd School, Lamotte Township and then the family moved to Kingston, Tuscola County, Michigan.

In May 2009 Charles McLaughlin (CHS 1966), the grandson of Whitney Hames, says he talked to an uncle that lives out of state and learned that "Whitney Hames graduated from Kingston HS. His brothers thought he was too lazy to go to work. He continued on to Michigan Normal (Eastern Michigan University). He went 2 years for a lifetime teaching certificate. His first job was supervision of student teachers at EMU. His next job was Superintendent of schools for Livonia, where he hired his future wife (Ethyl) and her good friend Fern. Fern married Ray West. The four of them were life-long friends. Later he taught for many years at CHS."

I found Whitney's draft registration. It was dated June 5, 1918, said he was 21 years old, and living in Clawson. It said he was born in 1897 in Troy Township. This was before the Village of Clawson was formed. It went on to say his father was George Hames of Clawson. George was born in Troy Township.

As a side note, Whitney's aunt, Rhoda Hames, sister of George Hames, married Allen "Allie" Hendrickson. The 1880 census shows that Allen & Rhoda were married and living in Troy Township. By 1900 they had followed her brother George and her father Hiram to Lamotte Township. The 1910 census shows that Rhoda was a "widow" and she and son Harvey were living back in Troy Township. I believe this to be on a farm at the present day Rochester Rd & Hendrickson Street.

James Hunter
CHS 1970
Dentist

Born on July 22, 1952, Jim Hunter is the oldest son of James & Ruth Hunter. His siblings are Robert (CHS 1971), Kathy (CHS 1973) and David (CHS 1978) Hunter. They grew up on John M Street in Clawson.

Jim received his Bachelor's degree from the University of Michigan (1974). He then went to University of Michigan dental school and received his dental degree (1978).

He is the only person I am aware of that grew up in town, became a dentist, and set up his practice in Clawson. He is married and has two children, Jimmy and Leah.

As to why he came back to his home town, he writes as follows:

> Upon graduation from dental school, I strongly considered hanging my shingle somewhere out West—but deep down I knew that my bond to the community of Clawson was too strong. My memories, family, and friends are what have always given my life meaning, so here I am in Clawson thirty years later and with no regrets.
>
> I am in the town nearly every day, and on each of those days I realize how thankful I am to be a part of the community. My memories are rich with examples of how individual volunteers, administrators, teachers, and other members of the community add to Clawson's vibrancy and maintain our tradition of a close-knit town.
>
> I am indebted to the people of Clawson on many different levels and for many different reasons, and for this I am extremely thankful.

Steven McClelland
CHS 1984
Physician

Steve McClelland is the son of Alan and Joan McClelland. Steve has a sibling, Jim (CHS 1979) McClelland. They lived on N. Manitou. Alan was a teacher, principal, administrator and retired from Clawson School system.

Steve became a medical doctor and he came to Clawson and set up a medical practice. He is only one of two people that I am aware of that grew up in town and set up a medical practice here. The other was Dr. Fred Reid, back in the late 1920s. Steve is also Director of Ambulatory Services at Royal Oak Beaumont Hospital.

Steve was a very good distance runner in high school. He has continued to run since then and has competed in triathlons, half-marathons and the Fire Cracker Mile that takes place just before the Clawson 4th of July Parade.

Frederick Reid
Physician

Fred Reid was born January 1896 in Clawson to Samuel and Jennie Reid. According to Deloris Kumler, retired-curator of the Clawson Historical Museum, the Reid's were an early Clawson family. According to the 1900, 1910 and 1920 census the Reids were living in Troy Township, Oakland County and the children were attending school. The 1910 census indicates they were living on a farm on Clawson Road (present day 14 Mile Road) in Troy Township. Census also indicated that Fred's siblings were a sister named Alta, Alva or Alba Reid (born in 1892), Glen H. Reid (born in 1895), and a brother named Samuel Raymond Reid or Raymond Samuel Reid (born in 1897).

According to Deloris Kumler, Fred was the first Clawson boy to get his medical license. He set up his medical practice in Clawson. Fred built a house at 47 Broadacre in 1928.

Bris Hunter (CHS 1943) said Fred was an Oakland County Health Officer. He was the one who visited sick people and put tags on their doors to quarantine people and indicating what their sickness was. Bris thought the tags were Red for scarlet fever, Purple for whooping cough, and Green for measles.

Fred was an examining physician for the U.S. Selective Service and practiced medicine until the 1960s. He died in 1968.

Clare Wilson (Volk), Helen Johnson, Lois MacDonald and Tom Cooper

Clair Wilson Volk

CHS 1931

CHS Teacher

Clair Wilson Volk was a member of the three person 1931 CHS Debate Team that won the Michigan State Championship that year. The other two people on the team were Helen Johnson and Tom Cooper.

On page 119 of Deloris Kumler's book *Clawson The Way It Was* is a photograph of the Debate Team along with CHS Principal/Team coach, Lois MacDonald. The Village of Clawson sponsored a civic dinner to honor the winning team. One hundred and fifty-eight people attended the banquet. Main speaker at the dinner was Professor G.E. Densmore, head of the public-speaking department at the University of Michigan. School Superintendent Charles Johnson and High School Principal, Lois MacDonald also spoke. Music was provided by the high school orchestra and Margaret Canfield sang a solo.

Clair Wilson was the daughter of George and Mary Wilson. According to the 1930 census Clair had one brother, Albert, four years younger than herself. George Wilson was an inspector at a auto factory. They were living at 236 Kinross.

Shirley Dittmar Wilson (CHS 1945) said Clair taught sociology and English IV and she was a "wonderful teacher." Clair Wilson went to Alma College as did John Volk, her future husband. John became principal of CHS and Clair taught there. WW-II broke out and John left CHS to join the military. Clair continued to teach. Enid Freeman took over as principal while John was away. When John came back from the war he took back his job as principal. Clair didn't think it was right for both her and John to be working in the same school, so Clair left Clawson and became a teacher at a Huntington Woods, Elementary School.

The second member of the Debate Team was Helen Johnson. According to the 1930 census she was the daughter of Charles and Minnie Johnson. There was one other sibling listed, Thomas, who was two years younger than Helen. The Johnson's were living at 68 Phillips and both parents were public school teachers. Mr. Johnson was probably the Charles Johnson mentioned above who was school superintendent.

The third member of the Debate Team was Tom Cooper. The 1930 census showed that he was the son of Charles and Edna Cooper. There was one other sibling listed, Betty, who was four years younger than Tom. They were living at 63 Baker. Dad was a traffic man for an auto factory and mom was a welfare worker for Oakland County.

Clawson to Clawson Teachers

In addition to the above mentioned people, the following is a list of Clawson students who came back to teach in the Clawson Public School System. Truly Clawson to Clawson.

Last Name	*First*	*Married Name*	*HS Year*	*Taught- Other*
Acton	Robert		Log Cabin 1945	Math-Coach-Administration
Baker	Debra	Smith	CHS 1970	Elementary
Baker	Peggy	Hauswirth	CHS 1972	Elementary
Bowen	Maryann	Markwick	CHS 1940	Taught in 40s & 50s & subbed
Dittmar	Shirley	Wilson	CHS 1945	Gym, coach, councilor
Gibbard	Ken		CHS 1954	Science, coach
Hames	Whitney		b. 1897 in Clawson. Moved away and then back to Clawson during his mid teen years. Teacher in Clawson & Principal at Clarenceville HS.	
Hauswirth	Erica		CHS 1999	Elementary
Joyce	Margie	Oberer	CHS 1982	Elementary
Kettlewell	Courtney		CHS 1997	Elementary
Luxton	Frank		CHS 1965	English, HS Principal
Mahaney	Denise	Kott	CHS 1992	Elementary
Markwick	Jill	Conaton	CHS 1968	Math
McDonald	Kelly	Horne	CHS 1996	English, coach
McGraw	Mike		CHS 1981	Social Studies, coach, athletic director

Moine	Linda	Wright	CHS 1969	Elementary
Morris	Ron		Morgantown HS 1949	Business, coach. He attended CHS up to 1948 when family moved WV.
Neider-schmidt	Irma	Anderson	CHS 1938	Elementary
Olin	Amy	Gjonaj	CHS 1999	AI Elementary
Reynolds	Laurie	Putnam	CHS 1977	Elementary gym, coach
Schram	Joann	Crocker	CHS 1969	German, English
Smith	Marisa	Reisdorf	CHS 1999	Elementary
Sparks	Jim		CHS 1985	Middle School, coach
Tantanella	Sadie	Hanes	CHS 1953	HS Secretary 1953 to present (2009)
Volk	Jeff		CHS 1965	Elementary
Wilson	Clair	Volk	CHS 1931	Taught 30s & 40s & in Huntington Woods
Young	Amanda		CHS 2000	Elementary

NOTABLES

Valdor (Les) Haglund
CHS 1967
Father of 2008 Miss America

Les and Iora Haglund are the parents of the 2008 Miss America, Kristen Haglund. They live in Farmington Hills, Michigan. Kristen's maternal grandmother is Lora Hunt, 1944 Miss Michigan.

Les wrote this just after Memorial Day 2008:

> Hi Everyone, Not sure that I know all of you but as a former 'Able Fighter' from the 6918th (Mar 69—71), I thought you might be interested in a little news from our family's front.
>
> My wife and I were this past weekend guests of the American Veterans Center in Washington DC for their annual National Memorial Day Parade. Our daughter Kristen (Miss America 2008) was in the parade with wounded vets and was one of the Grand Marshals along with actor Gary Sinese & Joe Montega. It was a wonderful event and we had the distinct honor of meeting three Congressional Medal of Honor winners (and Mickie Rooney).
>
> ...Besides my active duty Air Force days, I also was in the Army Reserve for 9 years and got out shortly after the 1st Gulf War in 1991 (Major, 0-4)."

Arthur Sunquest
Never attended school
Friend of the Clawson Police Department

Art was born April 1, 1925, the son of Glen and Fannie Sunquest. According to the 1930 Clawson census, Art was the youngest of six children. These were Dorothy M. (CHS 1934), Marian (CHS 1936), James S. (CHS 1938), Robert Guy (CHS 1939), Margaret (CHS 1942) and Art (never went to school). They were living at 143 W. Baker. Later they lived close to Frank Cribb (CHS 1947) who was living on Lincoln at the time. Cribb was the future Chief of Police in Clawson. Art was a dwarf and like many Little People of that time, didn't attend school. The families tended to keep the children away from the public. However, according to Frank Cribb, Art would run the streets at night. Frank recalled that his mother had heard kids outside creating a disturbance. She looked out and saw a group of teenagers down the street being very loud. She inquired as to who was leading the gang. Well, it was Art Sunquest. Art wore a leather jacket and one of his friends had painted "ART" on the back.

Art did become a very familiar person around town. He helped Johnnie Stone at the Ambassador Roller Rink, hung out at the bowling alley, rode his three wheel bike all over town, and was often seen riding in a Clawson Police car. Frank Cribb became Chief of Police in the early 1950s. He made sure that everyone watched over Art. Art would ride his bike to the police station nearly every afternoon and keep the desk officer company. On occasion he would answer the phone if it became busy. If the weather was bad a police car would pick Art up at his and his mother's home at the corner of Charlevoix and Custer and give him a ride to the police station. On occasion Art would go on patrol with the officers, helping out the best he could. Frank Cribb said that Art had helped him out numerous times while on patrol. Some people in town where just habitual complainers and usually complained about nothing. When Frank would answer these types of calls, Art would give him a few minutes and then yell to Frank that he had another call when actually no call came in. This would allow Frank to get away from the people without making them mad. When the Clawson Police began selling bicycle licenses, Art got the first number: 00001.

Art's mother died in May 1974 and Art lived in the Charlevoix home by himself. Art died in February 1981 from a staff infection that developed from a sore on the bottom of his foot. He had waited too long to get medical attention.

Art was a rough and gruff kind of person so he fit in very well with the officers. Art was the eyes and ears for the police department.

July 1, 2009, Don Witt (CHS 1948), son of one time Chief of Police, Clarence Witt, told me that Art had been a very good friend of his. Art "was a very good marble player" and "he cleaned up on everyone."

When I was a patrolman/detective on the Clawson Police Department from April 1966 to June of 1999, Art went on patrol with me many times—and helped me out of many scrapes using the police radio.

The Ullman Quads
CHS 1976
Quadruplets Born in Clawson

In October 1958 quadruplets (Helen, Martha, Marian and Catherine) were born to Chester and Julia Ullman, who lived on Hendrickson. This is many years before the first known in vitro fertilization baby was born, which happened in 1978. The Ullmans ended up with nine children in all. All the children graduated from Clawson High School. The first six had attended Guardian Angels School for elementary grades until it got to be too expensive to send them. They then started into public school.

The Ullman children are Charles (CHS 1974), Louise (CHS 1975), The quads Helen, Martha, Marian, Catherine (CHS 1976), Beatrice (CHS 1978), Paul (CHS 1980), and John (CHS 1982).

I, along with my wife, Barbara Fraser Hayes (CHS 1967), remember attending girl's basketball games at Clawson High in 1976. There were times when Clawson was far enough ahead or far enough behind that five Ullmans would be on the floor at the same time. It would be the Quads and Beatrice, who was a sophomore at the time, on the floor. The girls tried hard and always seemed to work up a sweat. They looked like they really enjoyed being out there.

On page 174 of Deloris Kumler's book *Clawson The Way It Was* has a photograph of the four girls in highchairs when they were about six months old. The text said "Folks were so excited about their birth a Ullman Quad Jamboree was held at the Ambassador Roller Rink. The planning committee of Johnny Stone, Shannon Dreon, Dick Avery and Bristol Hunter (CHS 1943) organized performers, a floor show and dancing. In addition all the civic groups and several businesses in town participated. The proceeds of $1.00 donation for all who attended, was given to the girls."

The VanderVen Brothers
Ned (CHS 1950)
Jack (CHS 1951)
Tom (CHS 1955)
Researchers/College Professors/Authors

Mary VanderVen (CHS 1962) wrote the following about her three brothers. "I have three older brothers, two of whom are PhDs and retired college professors."

"My oldest brother Ned VanderVen graduated from Clawson HS as co-valedictorian in 1950. He received his undergraduate degree from Harvard and his PhD in physics from Princeton in a program that went directly from a baccalaureate degree to PhD—no Master's. He was a professor of physics at Carnegie Mellon University in Pittsburgh from 1961 until his retirement in 2000. He is presently is a Professor Emeritus at Carnegie Mellon."

Ned wrote, "My past work has been primarily the application of microwave spectroscopy to the study of a variety of solids. These measurements have utilized both fixed and variable-frequency spectrometers."

Mary continued, "My middle brother Jack VanderVen graduated from CHS in 1951. He has a BA from Johns Hopkins and two Master's Degrees, one in history from the University of Michigan and one in library science from the University of Pittsburg. Jack taught for many years in both Michigan public schools and then in Michigan community colleges. After receiving his Master's in library science, he worked in Cincinnati in the city's library system until his retirement several years ago.

"My youngest brother, Tom VanderVen, was a member of the CHS class of 1955. He completed his junior and senior years at Phillips Academy Andover in Massachusetts. Tom graduated from the University of Michigan with both a BA and MA in English and received his PhD in English, from the University of Colorado. He taught at Indiana University, South Bend from 1967 until his retirement in 2001. He is now Professor Emeritus and teaches English part-time at the University of Georgia, where he also directs the writing laboratory for student athletes. Tom is also a published poet."

IN REMEMBRANCE

World War I

GILBERT DUNLOCK

Listed in D. Kumler's Clawson Book. Gassed during WWI and died 1922 of injuries. Was married to Viola Measel, b. 1903. She later married Frank Cribb's father. Cribb was Clawson's Chief of Police in 50s, 60s and 70s.

EARL W. MATTIMORE

Name listed on Clawson Memorial & in D. Kumler's Clawson Book. He was the only Clawson boy killed in battle in WWI; b. 1897; d. Overseas 29 June 1918.

World War II

There are over 30 names on this list of young men from Clawson or with connections to Clawson who died, were Missing In Action (MIA) or Prisoner Of War (POW) in World War II. This list came from several different sources. The main list of names came from the plaque at Memorial Park on the north side of the Clawson Library. Some of the other names came from Deloris Kumler's (Past Curator of the Clawson Museum) list, news clippings from the museum and private scrap books donated to the museum. A few of the names came from Robert Acton, Luella Dreon Joyce and Bristol Hunter who had personal contact with these people growing up.

This list is not complete. I'm sure there are names that should be on the list that aren't here because I'm not aware of them. When reading the newspaper clippings it looks like family members had to notify the newspapers if there was any news about their sons or daughters. Then someone had to save the clippings and share them with the museum in later years. The local American Legion & VFW Halls did not get notified by the government about any deaths, MIA or POW. They received their information the same way as everyone else, the local newspaper or rumor around town; so it is understandable why some people are not on the list.

- Most of the people grew up in Clawson, attended CHS and went into the service.
- Some others lived in Troy Township and attended Log Cabin High School or CHS, then went into the service.
- There is one name on the list that lived in Clawson and went to Saint Mary's High School in Royal Oak.
- There are several that lived in Clawson and then finished their senior year at the Ford Trade School.
- Two brothers probably lived in Clawson and one of them went to Longfellow School in Royal Oak, moved away and finished school in Kansas.
- Some others moved to town after they went to school and then went into the service. So they would be on a list in another county or state.
- Still others entered the service and their families moved away before there was any news about them.

ROBERT(?) BRUNDRIDGE

Name on D. Kumler's list at museum. Unable to find name on Oakland or MI casualty lists. Nor 1920 MI census list.

CYRIL E. BURRY

CHS 1940 — Army Air — Name in newspaper article — MIA and then POW in Germany — Lived 710 S. Main — Came home and married Emma Potts. He died in 1977.

JOHN O. CARTWRIGHT

101 Airborne — Army Pvt. — Name in newspaper article at museum — Lived 509 W. Baker — Died of wounds at Bastogno Sector, Belgium, 17 Jan 1945. Buried White Chapel. He was one of five from Clawson to die in the Battle of the Bulge.

WILLIAM H. CHAMBERS

CHS 1942 — Army — Name listed on memorial — Killed in action at Battle of the Bulge — He was one of five Clawson boys killed at Battle of the Bulge. Bris Hunter (CHS 1943) said Bill was an only child. Mother was so grieved she had to have another child. She had diabetes but gave birth to another son 24 years after Bill.

JOSEPH LEROY CLINE

CHS 1939 — USNR Name on memorial & in newspaper article at the museum — lived 1008 Grant — Mother Mrs. Helen Cline — Died in combat– aerographer's mate 2nd class — MIA South Pacific — Never found.

SAM B. D'ARMOND

CHS 1938 — Marine Corps — Staff Sgt — Name on memorial and many newspaper articles at museum — Parents Robert & Iola 103 Tecumseh — Bris Hunter says Sam died at Battle of Guadalcanal, his mother was the head of the Gold Star Mothers for the State of Michigan. — Gold Star Mothers is an organization of women who have lost a son or daughter in the service of our country — Bris said he played drums with Sam in the High School band.

WILFRED E. DONOHUE, JR

Log Cabin 1936 — Army Staff Sgt. — Name on memorial and newspaper articles at the museum — Killed in Action 16 March 1945 — Wife Alice Mae and 8 month old daughter — lived at 215 Madison — S/O W. E. Donohoe of 269 Fisher Ct and Mrs Peter Kembor of 96 School — Buried in Grand Duchy Cemetery, Luxemburg — Bris Hunter said Wilfred was married to Alice. After he died, she married Frank Darson. Alice Darson still lives in town (2009)

DELBERT ELMER DUFRAINE (SPARK)

USNR — Seaman 1st Class — Name in newspaper at the museum — MIA — since 30 July 1945 — Mother Bertha DuFraine, 590 Hendrickson — wife Margaret & five children.

ROBERT G. DYKE

2nd Lt. Army — Name in newspaper at the museum — MIA & then KIA in Germany — wife Rosemarie (Mouch) Dyke lived at 651 Goodale — s/o Mr & Mrs Curtis Dyke of Detroit. Robert was found on the Wayne County list.

GEORGE T. EASTMAN

Army PFC — Name on D. Kumler's list — Died of Wounds 1944 — Bris Hunter says that George died at the Battle of the Bulge, one of five Clawson boys killed at that battle.

DONALD E. ELLIS

CHS graduate per D. Kumler — Army/Army Air Force — Tec 5 — Name on D. Kumler's list — Died of non-battle related injuries and listed on casualty list for Oakland County — may have lived on E. Tacoma, Clawson

HERMOND FORD
(see also Hermond Lord)

Attended CHS — Name in newspaper article at the museum — Honor Roll list at CHS maintained by James Hunter, Sr — Bris Hunter says the name is probably LORD and not Ford. Lord's father was pastor of the Methodist Church in Clawson. There was a Hermon H. Lord found on Army casualty list for Wayne County.

MILTON FORD

Attended CHS — Name in newspaper article at the museum — Honor Roll list at CHS maintained by James Hunter, Sr. Milton listed as "undergrad" — Milton's name was not on Michigan casualty list. There is a Milton J. Ford from Michigan that died in 1944.

MAURIS W. GARDNER (MAURICE)

Army Pvt. — Name on D. Kumler's list at museum. Also name is in a newspaper article (dated 9-25-44) at the museum. Wife Mildred lived at 413 Allen, Clawson. He was KIA in Europe — Name found on Wayne County list.

HAROLD H. HENDRICKSON

Attended Log Cabin, Class of 1945 — Army Air Force — Sgt. Bob Acton (LC Class of 1945) said Harold left school early. His name shows up in a news article at the museum. KIA 28 Feb 1945 in Belgium. Acton said he was a tail gunner and he died on his first mission.

ALEX G. HILL

CHS 1938 — Private — Name on memorial, news articles at museum. He was listed as "undergrad" in one of the articles — Lived 288 Walper — Died in New Guinea

FLOYD A. HINMAN

CHS 1941 — Corporal — Name on memorial and news article at museum — KIA 16 Jan 1945 in Germany — father J. Bryan Hinman at 118 Nakota — Bris Hunter (CHS 1943) says Hinman was killed at Battle of the Bulge.

BERT HOWIE
(see also Bert Hubenet)

CHS 1936/37 — Bris Hunter said (2009) Bert was shot down in Europe or Africa and became a POW. He came home after his release. There was a Robert Howie at 128 Bauman. Bris didn't think he mixed Howie & Hubenet up but he wasn't positive.

BERT HUBENET
(see also Bert Howie)

CHS 1932 — Name in news article at the museum — MIA then POW in German Prison Camp. Family moved to Chicago before 6-2-1943 (date on article)

JAMES C. JOHNSON

Navy — Name on memorial and news article at the museum — Navy dive-bomber pilot — d. May 26, ?? in the South Pacific. Father was Elbert Z. Johnson, 28 Renshaw, former councilman & mayor of Clawson. Brother of Robert H. Johnson, also killed in WWII.

ROBERT H. JOHNSON

RCAF — Name in news article at the museum — Brother of James C. Johnson. Killed over Germany Sept. 1942.

HERBERT KILBY

Log Cabin 1941 — Army PFC — Name on D. Kumler's list and in news article at the museum. KIA 24 Jan 1945 in Belgium. Wife Joan & daughter from Clawson — Parents Mr & Mrs Herbert Whitechurch, Butterfield Street, Troy.

HERMOND LORD
(see also Hermond Ford)

There is a Hermon H. Lord on the Wayne County casualty list — Army Major. Bris Hunter (CHS 1943) says there was a Hermond Lord whose father was pastor of the Clawson Methodist Church at this time period. Hermond was a medical doctor in the Medical Corp. Bris also said Hermond died at the Battle of the Bulge.

NORMAN LOWNDS

CHS grad — Army Air (?) — 2nd Lt. — Name in news article at museum — POW at Stalag Luft 7-A near Munich, shot down Aug 1944 released May 1945. Played football at CHS — Married — Father, Frank Lounds of 138 Square Lake, Troy — Mother Mrs D.O. Haggitt of Lansing

PAUL A. MEISINGER

Attended Saint Mary's of Royal Oak — T. Sgt. — Name on memorial- Name in news article at the museum — KIA 22 April 1945 in Italy — Parents Charles & Bertha Meisinger, 131 Chocolay — Paul born 1920.

CHESTER A. MCCLURG

PFC — Name in news article at the museum — Killed April 1945 in Germany at the age of 26. Mother was Lenora Kirchen, 124 Leroy.

STANLEY OSGOOD, MD

Royal Oak — Name on memorial — Bris Hunter (CHS 1943) says Stanley set up medical practice in Clawson. He was very popular. He went into the service. He had throat cancer and was discharged a few months later. Bris sold Stanley a milk shake, at Hunter's Drugs. Bris learned the next day that Stan had died sometime through the night. Stan's parents were William H. & Maria Osgood of 521 N. Main, Royal Oak (1920). Luella Dreon Joyce said (2009) that Osgood was her doctor and he suffered from a goiter.

DALE REYNOLDS

CHS — Name in news article at the museum. He was on Honor Roll list (deaths) of CHS students maintained by James Hunter, Sr — Name not listed on Oakland/MI casualty lists. Dale may be Sgt. Arthur D. Reynolds, — Army — KIA — Oakland County list — Serial #16084071

HUGH M. RODGERS

Army Private — Name in news article at museum — Hugh died of wounds 20 Sept 1944 in Germany at the age of 32. Wife Susan Rodgers lived at 830 Hendrickson. He was on Wayne County list.

THOMAS C. SAMPSON

Army 2nd Lt — Name on D. Kumler's list — KIA, name on Oakland County casualty list.

LEWIS C. UHLER

Attended Clawson — PFC — Name on memorial and in news article at the museum. KIA 13 March 1945 in Mindanao, Philippine Islands at the age of 30 yrs. He was the son of John Uhler, 33 Church St — Brother of John Uhler, who was stabbed to death in the home Dec 1977 by Michael Wenrich, 15 yrs old.

KEITH WINTER

Army 2nd Lt — Name on D. Kumler's list — Name on Oakland County casualty list — Bris Hunter says Keith was the son of D.L. Winter, pharmacist at Winter Drugs — D. L. Winter was one of the last Village Presidents before Clawson became a city.

KOREAN WAR

JOHN ANTHONY CIMA

Staff Sgt, U.S.M.C. – Killed in Action 10 June 1951 at the "Punchbowl" near Chuchon, South Korea.

GROVER DEWOLF (SONNY)

Niles School and CHS. – U.S. Army Cpl. – Killed In Action 12 July 1951, from Oakland County. Born 1933. VFW Hall, Troy Post, named after him.

ALBERT SHANNON DREON (SONNY)

CHS 1947 – Sgt. U.S.M.C. – Anti-Tank Company MIA in 1950, never found. Luella Dreon Joyce's brother.

WILLIAM KARR HIGGINS

CHS 1948 – U.S. Army Private – Killed In Action 20 July 1950, near Taejon, South Korea. Lived on E. Baker. He went to CHS, rest of family went to Catholic School.

DAVID KENYON HOWCROFT

Niles School and CHS 1951 – U.S.M.C. Private – Died 24 October 1952 at Western Outpost, South Korea

VIETNAM WAR

JAMES RAY LAUDICINA

Ray Laudicina is listed on the memorial at Clawson Memorial Park but not in D. Kumler's book *Clawson The Way It Was*. The only Ray Laudicina found was James Ray Laudicina from Union Lake, Michigan. He was born 19 April 1946.

James died 9 Sept 1967 in Quang Tri, South Vietnam. He was a Sergeant in the U.S.M.C. James may have moved to Clawson just before entering the Marine Corp.

James name is engraved on the Vietnam Wall Memorial in Washington D.C., Panel 26E — Line 39.

JOHN ROBERT MILLER
CHS 1963

John Miller's name is on the memorial at the Clawson Memorial Park and also in D. Kumler's Clawson book. John was the son and oldest child of Robert and Margaret Miller. His siblings were Rick, Marty and Bill and they lived on W. Selfridge. John was drafted into the U.S. Army and was a Sergeant in the 1st Calvary Ambulance Division. He was killed by small arms fire on 21 Nov. 1968 in Tay Ninh, South Vietnam.

John's name is engraved on the Vietnam Wall Memorial in Washington D.C., Panel 38W — Line 28.

While in high school John played football, basketball and baseball. He was an outstanding basketball player and tied the single game scoring record of 36 points set by Gary Boss (CHS 1960) and season scoring record for CHS his senior year. John was an Evans scholar and went to Michigan State University and received a degree in Hotel Management.

A couple years after his death, Clawson High added the John Miller Award to their athletic awards ceremony. This award is given to the athlete who exhibited John's traits, good citizen, sportsmanship, student and athlete. It is still given as of 2009.

Ginny Schalm (CHS 1963) wrote in June 2009: I have a John Miller story: When we were in the 4th grade there was this big snowball fight in front of the house next to me—which was 2 down from John's. It was the boys against the girls. We built bunkers of snow. Bunches of kids were in this fight: John, Bob Birch, Pat Noble, me, Karen, and Ralph Petersen from a couple classes below us. Ruth says she was there, the Lynch boy-who's name I can't remember—it was the whole Selfridge/Phillips/Manitou neighborhood. The girls were losing, and they thought the boys were cheating by were throwing ice balls instead of snowballs. They really hurt. At our 40th reunion weekend, Bob fessed up to say that they put *stones* in the middle of each snowball! They did cheat—it just took 48 years for them to admit it!

SIDNEY RASNICK

Sidney Rasnick is listed on the memorial at the Clawson Memorial Park and in D. Kumler's book about Clawson.

Sidney McArthur Rasnick was born 23 Aug 1944. He was the son of Sidney Rasnick. Sidney was married.

He died of small arms fire on 13 Sept 1967 in Dinh Tuong, South Vietnam. His name is engraved on the Vietnam Wall in Washington D.C. Panel 26 E — Line 67. He was a Pfc in the U.S. Army.

KENNETH WILLIAM SCHAUBLE

Kenneth Schauble is listed in D. Kumler's book about Clawson, pg. 193. He is not on the memorial at the Clawson Memorial Park. Kenneth was born 23 Oct 1947 and died 6 June 1968 in Quang Tri, South Vietnam. His name is engraved on the Vietnam Wall in Washington D.C. Panel 59W—Line 14 . Ken was a Corporal in the U.S.M.C..

When he was in the 10th grade his family moved to New Jersey. Before that, however, his family lived on Gardner Street and he attended Parkland School, Guardian Angels, Clawson Junior High, and his 10th grade at the High School. In 1966 he graduated from Northern Valley Regional High School—Old Tappan, in New Jersey.

Following his death in Vietnam, the citizens of Closter, NJ dedicated a park in his honor. Ken's oldest sister, Cheryl Schauble Schumacher (CHS 1963) send us a copy of a part of that dedication ceremony.

> At 1:30 P.M. on Saturday, 3 June 2000, a park atop a hill in Closter, New Jersey, will be re-dedicated. Schauble Park was named to honor the memory and the sacrifice of

one of our own, Corporal Kenneth W. Schauble. Ken was a Squad Leader with the 2nd Platoon, "Echo" Company, 2nd Battalion, 26th Marines. He served at Khethe Sanh on Hill 861-A during the 1968 Tet Offensive, and he was later Killed in Action on 6 June, 1968 during an intense battle in "Leatherneck Square" near Con Thien. The date of the ceremony closely coincides with the 32nd anniversary of the day he and 13 other Marines died.

On the day of his death, the 2nd Platoon of Echo Company was on a security patrol when they engaged a large North Vietnamese Army force concealed in a bunker complex. After a pitched battle which lasted several hours and resulted in numerous casualties on both sides, the 2nd Platoon was cut off, nearly out of ammunition, and had only sporadic communication with one remaining radio. Realizing the only hope was to break out, Ken gave the order to "fix bayonets" and he led 2nd squad "over the top," on line, into the enemy bunker complex. While Ken was killed instantly when struck by a machine gun bullet, the 2nd squad pressed the attack, suffering near total casualties while bringing the fight into the enemy bunker complex, killing numerous NVA.

Jim Kaylor, the only survivor from 2nd Squad, said "Ken was one of the many brave hearts who died that day; 14 Marines were killed and 11 wounded. He was always one of my heroes because he was a bright and very brave man. Ken Schauble was a strong leader, tough as hell and he loved the Marine Corps!"

HAROLD SOTZEN

Harold James Sotzen is listed on the memorial at Clawson Memorial Park and in D. Kumler's Clawson book, pg. 193. "Jay" was the son of Harold and Katherine Sotzen. Jay attended CHS. Jay was the oldest of five children. His siblings were Michelle, David, Paul (CHS 1977) and Mary Ann Sotzen. They lived on Selfridge.

Jay was born 4 Nov 1948 and died from small arms fire, 24 Oct 1967 in Thua Thien, South Vietnam. He was a Lance Corporal in the U.S.M.C.

DAVID TAYLOR

David Taylor is listed on memorial at Clawson Memorial Park and in D. Kumler's Clawson book on pg. 193. Kumler said David was the son of Mr & Mrs Scheuer and they lived on Grove Street.

The only David Taylor from Michigan listed on the Vietnam Wall in Washington D.C. is David Bernard Taylor, w/m, b. 5 Oct 1947 from Detroit. At this point it is not known if this is the correct David Taylor or not.

DAVID VANDERCOOK

David Vandercook is listed on the memorial at Clawson Memorial Park and in D. Kumler's Clawson book on pg. 193.

David was the son of Ray Vandercook. His siblings were Karen (CHS 1961) and Lori (CHS 1971) Vandercook. David had married Debbie Godfrey (once a member of CHS class of 1965), just before he left for Vietnam. He was a PFC in the U.S.M.C.

David's sister, Karen, and the rest of the family had a large flag pole installed between the west side of the house and Custer Avenue, a short while after David's death. *The Royal Oak Dailey Tribune* came out, wrote a story and took a picture of the flag pole. The pole was there for many years.

About the Author
Bill Hayes
CHS 1963

[EDITOR'S NOTE: After collecting and organizing all the biographies shown in this book, we asked Bill to add one more–his own. As you can see, for achievement, it fits right in with all the others.]

I am the son of Hugh & Wanda Hayes and oldest sibling of Ray, Dolores, Don and Rhonda. We moved to 134 Redruth in Clawson just days before school started in August 1954. As I stood in line for the first time to enter the doors to Kenwood School (4th grade), a red-headed girl in line ahead of me said, "The third grade line is over there." That girl was Renee Foster and we have remained friends ever since. I have made many more friends in Clawson since then.

I attended Kenwood in 4th grade and then Clawson Elementary for 5th grade, as Kenwood only went to the 4th grade at that time. Then it was back to Kenwood for 6th grade as an addition had been put on the school. Then it was on to Clawson Jr. High for grades 7 thru 9 and Clawson High for 10 thru 12. The school atmosphere was different than it is now. In Jr. High, for example, we had a "gun club" overseen by teacher John Walli. Members of the club would bring their shotguns and rifles to school so they could go to the shooting range at Bald Mountain directly after school.

I really enjoyed going to school and playing sports. I played football, basketball and ran track. [1] My senior year of high school I was placed on the first team Class "B" All-State Football Team. Twenty-five years later I was awarded the 1987 Harvey Barcus Award for "Outstanding Achievement" by the Detroit News. It is an award given to a person from the All-State Team from 25 years previous that has given back to their community.

After high school I attended Alma College and Eastern Michigan University. In April of 1966, I joined the Clawson Police Department.

I was only on the force a couple weeks when we were dispatched to the 500 block of Roth for an animal call. Someone said there was a big cat under the hood of their car. We opened the hood and discovered an ocelot lying on the engine of the car. It had chewed a hole in the radiator hose of the car allowing the coolant to escape. The ocelot was about 46 inches long from nose to tail and turned out to be an escaped pet from someone living in Romeo.

Barb Fraser and I were married in November 1969 and we ended up having three sons, Kevin, Kyle and Eric. Barb and the kids all graduated from CHS.

In 1977 I was assigned to the Oakland County Killer Task Force which was investigating 5 homicides of children who were about 11 years old. Three months later I was assigned to the Detective Bureau of the Clawson Police Department where I was the Juvenile Officer and one of two detectives. It was suppose to be for 6 months but I was still there 22 years later when I retired in June of 1999.

Clawson is a wonderful place to live and raise a family. It has a small town atmosphere and a big heart, which is exhibited by the many people that have gone on to do some noteworthy and unique things.

---

[1] EDITOR: Bill fails to mention that in track he held a school shot-put record that stood for many years after his graduation.

Breinigsville, PA USA
24 September 2009
224667BV00001B/3/P

9 781934 757819